ON A GREEK ISLAND

GREECE

THE CYCLADES

PAROS

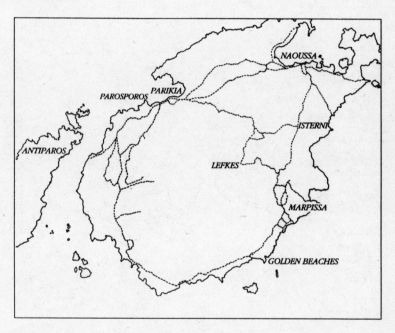

ON A GREEK ISLAND

A Personal Experience

FIONNUALA BRENNAN

POOLBEG

Published 1998
by Poolbeg Press Ltd
123 Baldoyle Industrial Estate
Dublin 13, Ireland

A catalogue record for this book is available from the British Library.

ISBN 1 85371 819 X

Cover design by Poolbeg Group Services Ltd
Set by Poolbeg Group Services Ltd in Goudy 11/14
Printed by The Guernsey Press Ltd,
Vale, Guernsey, Channel Islands.

A Note on the Author

Fionnuala Brennan was born in Tipperary and grew up in Belfast. She graduated in English and History of Art from Trinity College, Dublin and worked as a teacher in Zambia and Morocco. She has travelled extensively in Asia and spent several years in Greece where she wrote this book. She has two daughters and lives with her husband in Dublin.

Acknowledgements

I should like to express my thanks to the following: Faber and Faber for the brief quotations from Lawrence Durrell's *The Greek Islands*, (1978); Collins for the quotation from Ernle Bradford's *A Companion Guide to the Greek Islands* (1963, reprinted 1987). For reasons of privacy the names of some of the people in this book have been changed. My warmest thanks go to: John Pack, for his photograph of the Brennan family; Diana Murphy for the cover photograph; Kate Cruise O'Brien, my editor, for her encouragement and efficiency; and all the staff at Poolbeg for their good-humoured helpfulness.

For Rory, the best companion on any island, anywhere.

For Orla and Fiona, who were uprooted to live on Paros with us, and who love the island as much as we do.

For our many Parian friends, native and foreign, who made our lives on Paros so enjoyable.

For those friends I have mentioned and for all the other friends whom I have not been able to, not because their friendship is less valued, but because they did not live on Paros in those early years, which are the main focus of this book.

Contents

Chapter One

Serendipity

Beware of Greeks, even when they are not bearing gifts. For they are likely to tell you what you want to hear. "Paros is the best island in the Cyclades, the best island in the Aegean, the best in all of Greece," our travelling companions on the half-empty *Paros Express* insisted. "There's honey there and plenty of fish and apricots and oranges, almonds too and the best olives and wine, very good red wine, and *retsina* and lemons and *horta* and . . . and . . . everything. Marble, the whitest and purest in Greece, it's like glass."

"Where are you from?" I asked the dapper man with the excellent English who had translated for the rest of the passengers in the tourist-class salon.

"Paros," he replied. "I was born on Paros but I've spent many years in Australia. I'm coming home after twenty years. For me Paros remains the best place in the world."

"And this lady here. Where's she from?"

1

"Paros, too. She's a cousin of my mother's."

"All of you here are from Paros, isn't that right?"

"No, Dimitris is from Lesbos. But his wife's a Pariani."

On a cold, blustery day in November 1977 when the Boreas was whipping the sea into mountainous olive-green waves which hurled themselves against our ferry like battering rams, causing the passengers who were foolish enough to be standing to fall into the laps of those who were sitting, and bringing moans and prayers to the lips of the seasick ones, I desperately wanted to hear that we had finally come to our resting place. After three months travelling from island to island with my husband and two, small, exhausted daughters, I wanted to hear that the next island, which was still a distant shape on the undulating horizon, was for us. I longed for people to tell me that this island was the very place we had conjured up in our minds, the place we wanted to live in for a few years. I wanted to be assured that we wouldn't have to pack those blooming rucksacks again. Or get any more early-morning ferries. Or deal with any more seasickness. Or trail round any more villages with the baby buggy festooned with plastic bags, Rory and I bent under the weight of everything we needed to live in Greece for at least two years. Nor did I wish to bargain for any more cheap accommodation or have to live on eternal picnics of bread, olives, tomatoes, and cheese: food which could be prepared in a rented room on one plastic plate with a few plastic knives.

I had to beware not so much of Greeks telling me that their island was the best, but of believing that their island was the one for which we had been searching. For we had heard that Samos was the best, and then Kos and Kalymnos and Rhodes and Crete. And we had ferried

2

ourselves to these islands and indeed we had found many wonderful places and people, but not the place that we had dreamed of. Now we were sea-tired and our children were upset. They never knew where they would spend the night or what tension the next day would bring. The weather was getting colder by the day. Our rucksacks seemed to weigh kilos more every time we carried them onto buses and ferries. We were sick of traipsing around the Aegean on what sometimes seemed a useless search for what might only exist as an inner landscape.

But these Greeks were most insistent that Paros was for us. The old grandmothers who had lain on the red plastic banquettes, like figures on tombs in a cathedral, for the entire wind-tossed voyage from Piraeus suddenly came to life like people coming back to their senses after hypnosis as the ferry rounded the rocky spur of the island and slid into the calm waters of the bay of Parikia. It was as if some inner green light went on and they knew that it was now safe to sit upright. Nikos, our translator, was determined that everyone in the salon was to be consulted as to the suitability of Paros as a place of abode for a young Irish family. The grannies clucked and nodded and sucked in their breath and said that, of course, Paros was perfect, there were no gun-toting brigands as on Crete, no half-Turkish vagabonds as on Samos. Paros was the place for families; it had a good climate, plenty of pure water and it was safe. Paros had the famous Byzantine church of the Virgin, the Ekatonpyliani, and many monasteries. We were not ordinary tourists, they said, because we had children and we were travelling in winter and so we were respectable and serious, the kind of people they wanted on Paros. *Kalos elate!* Welcome! Welcome!

3

I went up on deck to see if something in the air would tell me they were right. If some wind messenger would whisper, "Welcome. Here you can rest. This is the island for you. Here your interior landscape has its external form."

The deck of the *Paros Express* was still streaming with water from the hill-high waves that had lashed the ship during the seven-hour voyage from Piraeus. The sea was the colour of wet Bangor blue slates and the town of Parikia hung in the distance like a beckoning promise. I listened again for wind messages. But the wind had dropped and all I heard was the sibilant swoosh of light waves against the prow and the noise of the ship's engines throbbing. I sniffed the air for the scent of the end of the search. The smell of salt, of seaweed, of the excitement and loneliness of sailors' lives, of rich catches of fish and of wind-borne thyme and oregano told me that this was a Greek island like so many others we had been on.

A sense of sudden certainty enveloped me like a warm shawl as I leaned over the cold railings and watched our ship's wake churn the sea aquamarine and white. It probably had its birth in wishful thinking, in fatigue, in a feeling that the time must be right because it was by chance that we had decided to come to Paros. It was a feeling born in the belief that nothing happens by accident and that serendipity was at work.

Our bright-orange, rusting, flaking, ex-Channel packet on its last sea legs, announced our arrival in the bay of Parikia with a series of horn blasts that echoed off the mountain behind the white port. As we drew nearer to the shore, the town unfolded itself along the coast. A necklace of white, cube-shaped houses, cafes, and shops was broken by the blue beads of church domes and by the spars of several windmills gesticulating like drunken exclamation marks. Behind the town, ink-blue hills, splotched with dark-green olive groves, rose to a crescendo in Mount Profitas Elias, which Nikos informed us was the highest peak on the island. Brightly painted caiques, those sturdy Greek fishing boats, rocked on the calm water of the port. Groups of fishermen sat along the quayside, their legs straight out in front of them, their heads bent in concentration over their brilliant orange nets, patiently untangling the knots and mending the holes. It was two o'clock in the afternoon; the sun had burnt away the morning mist and the famous Greek *phos*, that magical, sharp, clear light, lit the harbour like a stage set.

I went downstairs to the stuffy salon to collect my family and luggage for disembarkation, relieved that this time there would be no pushing and shoving to get down the stairs to the car deck and off the boat. Not many people travel for pleasure on Greek ferries in late November. Besides the four of us, there were a few dozen passengers on board the *Paros Express*, most of them merchants returning with truckloads of supplies for the island's shops. These men had spent the long journey playing noisy games of backgammon and smoking ceaselessly, casting a confetti of abandoned cigarette butts on the floor around their feet. Rory had stoically continued reading Pausanias's ancient guidebook to Greece while I read out bits about modern Paros from our guidebook to whoever cared to listen and tried to distract our children from being seasick with long, complicated stories and bags of glucose sweets. I was not entirely successful and had to make several sudden dashes with a

5

green-faced child to the stinking ship's toilets or to the heaving rails.

When the grinding sound of the anchor being lowered over the side of the ship could be heard and the throttle of the engines ceased, the three old grandmothers in regulation black clothes rose to their feet and crossed themselves and murmured *Panagia mou* prayers to the Virgin Mary, thanking the Mother of God for delivering them safely to their families on Paros.

The waters of the bay were blessedly calm as we staggered down the gangway on rubbery legs, overburdened with our luggage and trying to hold the children by the hand to prevent them from slipping between the ropes and into the sea. We said goodbye to Nikos before he was engulfed by a crowd of excited relatives. The grannies were borne away by burly grandsons in pick-up trucks and we were left alone on the dock.

A short man with the shoulders of a mule was pushing a handcart along the dockside. He approached us as we stood indecisively beside our mound of luggage regaining our land legs. "Rooms rooms?" he smiled and we accepted his offer of finding us accommodation. He loaded our rucksacks, the mound of plastic bags, five-year-old Orla and her teddy bear onto the handcart. We strapped an unwilling Fiona into her baby buggy and followed Dimitris out of the harbour. He led us past a windmill with broken sails which marked the entrance to the village, along narrow, flagged streets, past small, dazzlingly white churches, on through the shade of pine trees intoxicating with resin, to the edge of Parikia where he found us a room in the house of his uncle and aunt, an old couple, Kyrios Giorgos and Kyria Eleni.

It was low season and we may have been regarded as an

unexpected and welcome late crop of tourists, so the nightly rate for our large clean room which overlooked a well-cultivated garden was really cheap. The old woman clucked over our children, pinched their cheeks (which they hated) and gave them a Greek treat for children consisting of a lump of sticky white vanilla in a glass of water (which they liked). Kyrios Giorgos took us into his garden and filled our arms with the fruits of his labours.

After a short rest to restore equilibrium, we set off to find out what sort of place we had landed in. We found a village which was a labyrinth of narrow marble-paved streets lined with small whitewashed houses like sugar cubes. Their balconies and steps, window ledges and courtyards were filled with flowers planted in blue, recycled, olive-tins. Arching purple and cardinal red bougainvillaea splashed the uneven white walls. Robust geraniums, white, pink, and red, thrived in every corner. Sky-blue doors and shutters did not shut out the domestic sounds and smells, the shrill Greek dance music on the radio, the calling of mothers to their children to come here and eat (*"Eleni, Dimitris, Mikalis, elate edo!"*), the animated family discussions, the smells of garlic, fish, squeezed lemon juice and olive-oil on sizzling frying-pans. There was another scent also, that of pungent incense and candle-wax wafting from the open doors of the tiny churches which seemed to be on every street corner, like pubs in an Irish town – a nostalgic smell for Irish Catholics brought up in the fifties and sixties. But these sounds, smells, sights were common all over Greece. What was so significant about Paros? Why did I feel so certain that this was the island for us?

I began to understand why as we walked on through the village and along the seafront. Everything we saw and experienced matched my inner landscape, our ideal Greek island. It was a magical combination of features: the small scale of the place, the simple, low, white, flat-roofed houses, the narrow traffic-free streets, the unhurried village atmosphere, the sandy beaches we had seen from the ferry, the defiant decrepit windmills, the tiny unpretentious churches with their blue bulbous domes and marble lintels, the absorbed fishermen, the gentle hills, the flowering courtyards, the donkeys carrying creels of vegetables and fruit, the smells of good cooking and candle-wax. The domestic simplicity of the place. Paros was not important, busy, and touristy like Rhodes. Nor was it large and faintly intimidating like Crete. Paros was the island we had dreamed of for a year while we worked and saved in dear damp Dublin. This was the island where we could live happily for a few years with our children. We recognised it and delighted in the finding.

Back in Dublin, months before, we had drawn up a list of quite specific requirements. The island where we would live would have to have sandy beaches: children do not like rocky shores, they cannot build sandcastles on pebbles. There also had to be a plentiful supply of fresh fruit and vegetables, a doctor, some amenable company, and a house to rent near the sea. Of course, this island also had to be very beautiful in a gentle way. We were sure we would know it when we saw it.

For this we had resigned our teaching jobs at the age of thirty and for this we had uprooted our children. For this we had, once again, worried our parents, who were concerned that we had not put our nomadic ways behind us, even after we had bought a house and had children and had seemed to settle down at last. But we wanted to do so many things before we were too old or too tired or just too drained. We did not want to wait until retirement age. We wanted to have time to write, to paint, to read philosophy, to make pots, to learn to spin and weave, and to play with and enjoy our children while they were still young.

As we walked through the streets of Parikia, watching our children run excitedly in front of us, absorbing the peaceful atmosphere of the back streets, returning the friendly *Kali meras* from old ladies sitting knitting at their open doors, I thanked the *I Ching* for directing us here. And I congratulated myself for following its advice, for trusting my instinct. I was heartily glad that we had both persevered in our weary search.

The gap between perseverance and stubbornness is sometimes quite narrow. Three months of vain searching with two young children is close to stubbornness.

We spent the month of September on Samos, an island which we found to be gentle and green but unfortunately full of soldiers perpetually waiting for a Turkish attack from the nearby mainland. Every taverna or kafeneion we went into was overflowing with men in uniform. It was like being in an exotic Northern Ireland. It was too familiar for comfort, especially for someone from Belfast like me. October saw us in spectacular medieval Rhodes of the Crusaders. We went there because we knew someone who knew someone who had a house in Lindos. They might be able to help us find what we were looking for. There were, and still are, magical places in Rhodes, wonderful houses with pebbled courtyards of intricate mosaics, lovely beaches, spectacular views. But even in late October the island was touristy; queues of people filed up to the acropolis in Lindos, past the women selling exquisite handmade lace and embroidered tablecloths.

Lindos was not the quiet village we were looking for. Besides, the friend of the friend had gone away for a while, his neighbour told us, and we had no inside information to help us find somewhere affordable to live.

We moved on to Crete in November, convinced that this was where we would find the place we were looking for. November weather can be chilly in Greece and it was, according to the Cretans, extra cold that year. Our children wore layers of clothes and we dug out our winter sweaters from the bottom of rucksacks. We took buses along the coast from Heraklion to Chania, we went up into hill villages and still we did not find what we were looking for. The lovely villages were up in the hills, far from the sea and we did not think we could survive the heat of the Cretan summer without the sea. The coast was full of tourist resorts, which we definitely did not like, and of towns, some of them interesting and pretty like Chania or Rethymmon, but there was no point in moving from Dublin to live in a noisy Greek town. In these three months of incessant and frustrating travelling, Orla and Fiona had become a little distressed, never knowing where they would wake up, and they missed home and grandparents. The poor children craved security and a place to stay and to play. At the end of November, with Christmas not too far off and nowhere to live, the whole family was travel-weary and losing hope.

At a very low point in Chania, the capital of Crete, we were sitting morosely on the bed in a dingy room lit by a forty-watt light bulb. Rain drizzled down the dirty windowpane and the broken shutters banged forlornly in the wind. Outside, a tin can rocketed aggressively from one side of the street to the other. We had come to a crossroads and there were no signposts to anywhere. Decision time.

Our choices came down to three. To rent the house we had found a short distance outside Chania, to move on to yet another island and start another search there, or to give it all up as a bad job and go back to the warmth and security of our home in Dublin.

The drawbacks of the house to rent in Chania were obvious, even to people desperate to settle somewhere before the winter. It was damp, dark, and right on the main road. There was a beach nearby, a clean sandy one, but the noise of traffic drowned out the waves. We resisted the choice of going back to Ireland, of facing family and friends after our grand, adventurous departure. Besides, there were tenants with a year's lease renting our house in Dublin. That left the final choice, of going on with the search. But the weather was getting colder and we were afraid of throwing good time after bad. What was there to say that we would be any luckier if we set off to yet another island? Perhaps it really was time to face up to the fact that reality and dreams rarely match.

At the bottom of a self-pitying well, I turned to the *I Ching* as to prayer. Many will know about the *I Ching*, the three-thousand-year-old Chinese book of oracles, which informed Taoist and Confucian philosophies and influenced the psychologist Jung. The basic theme of the *I Ching* is that continuous change and transformation underlie all existence. I use it when I am desperate, confused, when I cannot find a solution to my problems.

Rory was reading a bedtime story to the children. Orla was struggling to keep her eyes open until the end of the story while two-year-old Fiona had already dropped her little round head on the pillow and was sleeping like a cherub. I tried to formulate the most succinct question about our present dilemma to put to the *I Ching*.

11

For anyone not familiar with the *I Ching*, it is somewhat difficult to explain how it works. Basically you compose a direct question about your problem. For example, you cannot ask, "Should I do this or should I do that?" Rather you must ask, "Should I do this?" Then, concentrating all the time on your question, you throw three coins in the air. Let's say that you get two heads and one tail. According to the *I Ching*, heads are yin and have the value two. Tails equal three and are yang. So now you have got seven. The number seven is depicted by an unbroken line. Next time you throw the coins, say you get two tails and one head, equalling eight. The number eight is depicted by a broken line. You go on throwing the coins six times in all and drawing your broken or unbroken lines according to what number the heads and tails add up to. Your final hexagram will be one of the sixty-four in the *I Ching*.

Fifty-two was the number of the hexagram which my coins produced that day in Chania in answer to my question: "After all these months of searching in vain for our ideal place to live, is it time now to give up and go back to Ireland?" *Heng* (Duration) is the name of hexagram fifty-two. The relevant commentary read:

"Duration brings about firmness of character. Duration. Success. Perseverance furthers."

I interpreted the oracle to mean that we should endure, that we should go on with the search for our ideal home and that if we persevered we would be successful. We would not rent that noisy, damp dump of a house. We would not go home with our tails between legs, we would persevere.

"All right," said Rory, kissing the sleeping Orla, "but what exactly do you propose we do now?"

"We'll find a stepping-stone, another island with good ferry connections to several others. We'll go there, one of us will stay and look after the children while the other continues the search. That way we'll minimise the hassle of transporting all this luggage, and the children will be delighted to stay in one place for a while. We'll all be less tired and frazzled and we *will* find what we're looking for. I'm sure of that."

So we laid out our battered map of Greece on the floor and found Paros. An island in the Cyclades, it seemed to be on quite a few shipping routes. The next morning we once against stuffed things into bulging bags, strapped Orla's small rucksack containing teddy and her pyjamas onto her back, tied Fiona into her baby buggy, hung plastic bags of nappies and other emergency supplies on the handles and set off for the bus station in Chania. From Heraklion we endured another overnight ferry journey to Piraeus. There we just managed to catch the early morning boat to Paros. And here we were, convinced that the stepping-stone would turn out to be the very island we had been looking for.

Chapter Two

Villa Ariadne

"I am Captain Peter, who are you?" A stooped white-haired figure sitting at the next table and wearing a sea-captain's cap, leaned toward us and introduced himself. We were sitting at a kafeneion at the seafront having a rest and an ouzo, watching the sun hanging like a crimson lantern over the bay.

"Where you are from? Oh, Ireland! My wife, she was Irish too. Welcome in Paros. What you are doing here? We do not have much tourists now."

We managed to slip a few words of reply past the barrage of his questions. Captain Peter seemed to be more interested in his own rapid-fire questions than in our answers.

"Come to my house for some island *krasi*, you know, wine, then maybe some Captain Peter's soup, famous soup, from fish. Please come now. We go, yes? Is not far my house, very near."

Faced with such insistent hospitality, we could not refuse his invitation. We called the reluctant children from the beach and followed our captain.

Sitting on the bum-pinching wooden chairs at a tiny oilcloth-covered table in Captain Peter's kitchen, in front of brown earthenware bowls of his famous fish soup, we told him that we were looking for somewhere to live for a year or so. "Somewhere near a sandy beach for the children, in the countryside, if possible. Not too far from a village, as we have no transport. Is there a doctor on the island? One who can understand a little English, perhaps?" We railroaded our questions through a pause in the captain's monologue while he was busy cutting bread with a dangerous-looking knife.

Captain Peter was ecstatic. He rubbed together hands like flaccid flat fish, "You are in a lucky day. I have friend, Captain Yannis, he have four, maybe five houses beside the beach, only eight, nine kilometres from Parikia. Beautiful. You will see."

We finished the soup, drank several small glasses of sweet dark red wine and tried to stem the flood of his talk for long enough to make some concrete arrangements to go to see the properties. But Captain Peter was under full sail. In his anxiety to talk his words tumbled out, his voice rose as if he were in the crow's-nest of a ship in a storm. We resigned ourselves to wait until his fervour wore itself out. The man seemed starved for company and determined to amuse himself with his captured crew.

The restless children were sent into the street, to a shop at the corner where they could buy ice cream. Although the captain talked incessantly, we did not find out much about his Irish wife, only that her mother was Irish, her father Greek, that she was called Kathleen, and that she

16

was dead. Captain Peter was not a Pariano. He was a native of Piraeus and belonged nowhere, having spent most of his life aboard Greek merchant ships, before retiring to Paros, where his friend and old shipmate, Captain Yannis of the many houses lived. He had no relatives on Paros and he did not mention children.

Finally, the old man tired of his own voice and we were able to make some arrangements and to extract ourselves from his land cabin. We were to meet the two captains the next morning at eleven o'clock. Captain Yannis would be in a yellow Ford and would take us to view his houses at Agia Irini. "Saint Irene." *Irini*, the Greek word for peace. A good omen, surely.

It was dusk when we made our way back to our room. I felt peaceful, full of hope that the next day would bring us to the place we had searched for. I started singing in my tuneless way, as I always do when I am happy, until Rory and the children begged me to stop. Children are marvellous barometers of atmosphere: they picked up our excitement and took off like wound-up mechanical toys, skipping, running and squealing with delight. We had to tell them long, long stories to get them to sleep that night.

Before eleven the following morning we had located several greengrocer shops, a pharmacy, a sign for a doctor's surgery, several banks, the post office, and two tavernas still open after the summer season.

We waited for our two captains in what was to become our Parikia salon. Dinoasaki's kafeneion was on the *paralia* – a broad strip of street running along the waterfront. Its shiny, hospital-green walls, straw-seated wooden chairs and small, round, tin tables were replicated in thousands of cafes all over Greece. Over the bar in Dinosaki's hung a large photograph portrait of a stern-faced, bearded man whose dark ponytail was tied back under the black stovepipe hat of a priest. "My father," Dinosaki told us, "very holy man", as he served us our bitter coffee, called Turkish elsewhere but Greek coffee here. The children had *risogallo*, rice pudding sprinkled with cinnamon, which they loved. The era of junk food had not yet arrived on the island. We learnt afterwards that if Dinosaki had not liked the look of us, we would have been directed out of his cafe to the one next door.

Dionasaki chose his customers carefully. People who did not meet his standards were never served. Nobody knew exactly what these criteria were, as there did not seem to be any consistency. Some of his regular customers, the foreigners, were young and single, quite hippy in dress and manner.

Others, who looked the same to all intents and purposes, were refused service. He would put up with children only if they behaved themselves in his kafeneion.

Only twenty minutes late, a battered yellow car splattered with patches of rust-coloured repairs and bearing Captains Peter and Yannis, drew up outside the kafeneion. All four of us squeezed into the back seat and Captain Yannis drove unsteadily along the seafront. The suspension of the ancient car protested under its burden as we climbed up by a windmill, high on a small hill overlooking the bay, then out of Parikia, past vineyards, past orange and lemon groves, past scattered, white farmhouses sheltering behind their vine and bougainvillaea-draped terraces. It was one of those magnificent, heart-warming, Mediterranean winter days, the air clear as the pipes of Pan, the welcome lingering heat of the sun massaging your bones, and everything etched sharply on the day's copperplate.

We passed a dry river-bed along whose banks paraded a

18

procession of oleander bushes. The old Ford climbed for a mile or so, grumbling and snorting like a pensioned-off mule, before turning off the main road onto an ochre-coloured rocky track which led in sweeping s-bends to the sea about two kilometres below. Down the teeth-rattling road we clattered, the suspension of the car now screaming in agony, its pain no doubt exacerbated by Captain Yannis's daily journey to Agia Irini to see to his family's houses and lands which stretched around the shore.

"Here we have five houses. Any one you like, you choose," Captain Peter translated for his friend. And there, right there, in front of us and all around us, the dream scene we had conjured up and held onto for almost a year materialised before our delighted eyes. A sickle-shaped, glowing gold, sandy beach backed by tamarisk trees. A solid, square, two-storeyed white house with tall windows and faded blue shutters whose narrow first-floor balconies and patched wooden front door faced the sea. The house, which was about a hundred years old, was shaded along its entire length by a verandah festooned with bougainvillaea and vines. That was the first of Captain Yannis's houses. The second was some distance behind that, a little further inland. The third and fourth were set among vineyards along the bay and the fifth was near the tiny church of Agia Irini on a promontory at the far edge of the bay, looking across at the island of Antiparos.

Perfect. Paradise. A dream revealed. Thank you *I Ching*. Thank you my stubborn streak that refuses to give up a chase. Spoiled for choice, we walked from house to enchanted house, half-afraid to believe our luck. Here, at last, on Paros was everything we had dreamed of while we made extra money by selling bric-a-brac at our stall on damp freezing Saturdays in the Dandelion Market in Dublin.

As Adam and Eve found out, Paradise has its problems. We decided to rent the first house, the one with the verandah by the beach and started financial discussions via Captain Peter. Captain Yannis was not as green as he was cabbage-looking. The rent he mentioned was a lot higher than we had expected and much higher than the rent of houses we had looked at in Crete. Still, we wanted the place so much, we thought that, with a little bit of bargaining and a lot of economising, it might be possible to afford it. Captain Yannis came down by about twenty percent and we agreed to take the house.

"Oh, goody, goody," squealed Orla. "I like this beach. Come on, Fifi, let's make castles."

"Until June," Captain Peter said, having conferred once more with Yannis.

"June!" we repeated like startled parrots. "Why only until June? We understood the rent we have just agreed was for one year."

"Oh, is not possible," said our interpreter. "Captain Yannis, he uses this house as taverna in the summer, so you must to move out then."

We looked at each other. Rory nodded. "Then we'll rent the house beside the church," I said.

More conversation between the Greek captains. "That one also until June. Captain Yannis's brother, he rent it to a German woman. She come every summer, three months."

The other three houses were similarly only available until the summer when various members of the captain's family would arrive for holidays from Athens and Thessalonika. We could not take the risk of renting any of these idyllic houses for the winter and spring months and then having to find suitable cheap accommodation for a whole family in the high season.

20

"Well," we consoled each other on the journey back to Parikia, "maybe it wasn't that practical, anyway. It's five miles out of town. And that steep, rocky track would wreck the baby buggy in no time. And how could we have managed to do the shopping without a car? And, really, mightn't it have been a bit lonely out there on short winter days, without electricity or neighbours?"

Nonetheless, I looked back along the winding ochre road to the sea and felt deflated, the air gone from my balloon of joy. "Mammy and Daddy will find us another house, don't worry. Yes, with a beach. And nice flowers," we consoled the disappointed children.

"That's where the Englishman lives." Captain Peter gestured towards a snug farmhouse built into the side of a hill halfway along the road back to Parikia.

"So, there are some foreigners living on Paros?" we asked.

"Yes, many," was his reply. "The Englishman has a wife, beautiful, and one, two children. He makes statues. There is also American woman, name Deborah, a painter. She live somewhere near to here. Also some Germans, maybe also peoples from Hollandia, they live on Paros."

The rest of that day Rory took buses to other villages on the island, searching for houses to rent. He came back in the evening with stories of greedy landladies quoting rents at high-season nightly rates, of farmers who wanted to rent their stables as houses, of an impossibly low monthly rent, the equivalent of the cost of four loaves of bread, asked by a timid woman in the half-deserted village of Marpissa. "The house was a dark and damp hovel," he conceded, "and maybe she didn't understand me properly."

The following day I travelled around the rest of the island, while Rory looked after the children. It is not at all easy looking for a house to rent when you do not speak a word of the language beyond *Kali mera* and *Yiassou* and the words for please, thank you and goodbye. I had looked up the Greek words for house and year in my phrase book. *Spiti?* I asked in shops and kafeneions. *Ena kronon?* I was taken to tumbledown ruins, which I finally understood were for sale. I was directed to boarded-up houses for which neither the owners, their agents, nor keys could be found. I was shown tourist rooms at high-season tourist prices. Having walked the deserted streets of the hilly village of Lefkes, exhausted possibilities in the decaying fishing-port of Naoussa and going as far away as the summer resort of Drios, all to no avail, I gave up. On this island where we had so tantalisingly found so many bits of our dream jigsaw, the final and most necessary piece, that very basic human need, a place to shelter, eluded us.

"Hold firm," Rory and I exhorted each other that night. "We mustn't give up now. We've come so far, there *must* be somewhere for us on this island. It feels so right."

But, lying awake, each of us pretending to be asleep, we did not feel at all confident.

Before any of the family had woken the next morning, I was up and off. Cocks were crowing in the misty, early light, donkeys and hobbled goats rustled as they grazed ghost-like in glistening stone-walled fields. The sweet clang-clang of goats' bells and the incomparable Aegean light on the sea lifted my spirits once more like a seagull on a thermal current. No wonder, I thought, this island was a favourite of the poet Seferis. Once more I felt the light cloak of certainty on my shoulders and I resolved to stick with Duration.

As I walked up the bright morning road out of the town, I pondered again the particular charm of this rocky island. Here was beauty on a human scale. Unlike the more dramatic scenery of Rhodes or Crete, this landscape had a feminine quality, with gently rounded hills breasting the horizon. The satisfying, round, blue domes of small white churches dedicated to local saints in the memory of dead family members blessed the coastline. This island had a warm, embracing, maternal spirit. Moreover, there were echoes of home, of my favourite parts of Ireland, the untamed, rocky, western coasts of Cork and Kerry, Galway, Clare and Donegal. Dry-stone walls divided treeless fields here also and small whitewashed cottages looked out to sea, their backs turned to the prevailing wind.

Paros was enchanting and I was totally charmed by her, as was that modern Hellenophile Lawrence Durrell. Like me, he had asked himself what the charm of Paros was and he decided that the secret of her attraction was "the feeling of zestful ease it gives you when you navigate those dazzlingly white streets . . . its unexpectedness. Every day when you awake, it seems quite fresh, as though finished in the night and opened to the public, just this morning." Exactly.

Even without a home, I felt at home here. Arrived. Resting on a low wall which wrapped itself like a stone skirt round a wayside church, I exulted in my good fortune to be alive in such a place on such a morning as this.

After another mile or so I came to the hill where Captain Peter had pointed out the house of the English sculptor. At the end of a steeply rising donkey-path I came across a pretty blonde woman, about my own age, hanging out clothes on a washing-line stretched between olive-trees.

"Excuse me," I panted, getting my breath after the climb, "I've been told that an English family lives here, is that you?"

23

Phoebe looked somewhat startled by this early morning English-speaking intrusion. Yes, she said, she and her husband Clive and their two children had been living on the island for about a year.

Over a cup of herbal tea on the verandah she told me the rest of their story. Clive, a sculptor, had chosen Paros because of the quality and translucency of its marble. She told me that Parian marble was highly prized in ancient Greece and that Phidias had used it for the statues in the Acropolis in Athens. The ancient marble mines at Marathi were closed, she went on, but you could still go down the shafts and sometimes find pieces of marble big enough to work. The island was full of marble. Life was good on Paros, she assured me, you could live simply and quite cheaply. Their children were happy here. It was a healthy lifestyle. Yes, there was a doctor who spoke some English. And yes, Captain Peter was correct, there was a small foreign community, mainly painters and writers.

Then the big, the burning, question. Did she know of any houses to rent? *Mirabile dictu*, she did! Had I noticed a small villa set among orange-trees on the right, just before a track going down to the sea, about a mile back towards Parikia? The place was called Parosporos. Well, that had been Judy the painter's house and she had just left to return to Chicago. Petros, one of the butchers in Parikia, acted as a sort of a letting agent for the house because the old man who owned it was about ninety and did not speak any English.

At this point the rest of the Wheeler family appeared and I was invited to join them for breakfast which consisted of home-made yoghurt, bowls of fruit and honey, chunks of coarse-grained farmers' bread and Earl Grey tea. Their two children, a boy and a girl with white-blonde hair and ice-blue eyes were around the same age as ours. I could already see them playing together. Clive was a tall, thin, balding man, who spoke quickly and decisively. As he spoke, he gesticulated mildly with sensitive long-fingered, piano-player's hands which looked as if they were used to hard manual work. He had the manner of someone who had lived when most of the map of the world was coloured the red of the British Empire on which the sun never set. You could imagine him in another century sipping tea on a plantation in Ceylon while servants in starched white uniforms waited on the shady verandah. If I could wait for a half an hour or so, he would be going into Parikia to get some supplies and I could take a ride with him. Then we could go to look for Petros and find out if the house at Parosporos was for rent.

We rode into the village on a peculiar vehicle. It was an open, three-wheeled affair with a long steering column operated by what looked like bicycle brakes and connected to a small front wheel. The driver and one passenger could perch on a narrow bench seat. Behind the bench was a sort of trailer where one could carry sacks or luggage or even a few goats. It was, in fact, a mechanical plough, which doubled as a means of transport, albeit a very slow one. Somehow, crawling along the road at this agricultural pace suited my mood and the temperament of the island. No need to hurry in a timeless place. Apart from Captain Yannis's yellow banger and one or two grey taxis, I had not seen any cars on the narrow, pot-holed main road. On the way into Parikia we trundled past farmers riding sidesaddle on their laden donkeys, their heels clicking rhythmically on the donkeys' sides, taking their produce to sell at stalls in the village square.

Petros emerged from the back of his shop wiping

25

bloodstained hands on his butcher's apron. A tall, unexpectedly blue-eyed, fair, curly-haired Greek, he looked like a young Adonis. He had that reputation, too. Apparently, in the summer season he was kept very busy indeed, making *kamaki* with besotted foreign tourist girls. *Kamaki* is the Greek name for the short harpoon used by fishermen who dive to spear fish. It is also the main occupation of the island Lotharios from May until the last tourists depart in October.

I jiggled with impatience while Petros and Clive exchanged the necessary pleasantries. As in Ireland, it is not polite to come directly to the point in Greece. That would be too cut and dried, too precipitous and lacking proper rules for human intercourse. At last, Clive broached the reason for our visit and for my introduction to Petros. The news was good. The little villa at Parosporos was for rent. He would take us to meet old Cosmas Nomikos, the owner, as soon as he closed the shop for lunch.

It is not often in life that one gets exactly what one wants when one wants it. The feelings I experienced when I heard that the villa was for rent fluttered and flew from my stomach up my oesophagus and out of my mouth with a totally satisfied "Ah". And I understood something of what TS Eliot meant in his poem, "Journey of the Magi", by the phrase, "It was (you may say) satisfactory."

Rory and the children were still asleep when I burst into our room to tell them of my early-morning adventures. It was the first lie-in they had had in months and they needed the rest. My family got up without protest when they heard the news. We spooned yoghurt and fruit into the children and gobbled a hunk of bread and cheese each. Bundling Fiona and teddy into the baby buggy, we quick-marched Orla the three kilometres to the villa at

26

Parosporos as if it might disappear if we did not see it immediately. It was love at first sight.

The house was built in the early 1930s in the style of a small rectangular villa with a wide front door, flanked by wall niches. Peering through the curtainless windows, we could see intricately-patterned coloured floor-tiles similar to those in old country churches in Ireland. The walls were whitewashed, the ceilings lofty and wooden-beamed. An enormous eucalyptus tree shaded the entire front of the house where a great stone slab had been mounted on a cement base to form a table on the marble-flagged terrace under the tree. The house was built below the road and approached by foot-sized steps that descended from a stone wall which surrounded the vineyard in front of the house. The land sloped at the back of the house so that the garden was higher than the fields beyond it. It was a magic place of orange and lemon-trees and of tall geranium bushes. A swaying, swishing bamboo fence protected the garden from the sea breeze. A picture-postcard stone well with a winch to pull up buckets of springwater stood in the middle of the garden.

From the narrow verandah outside the back door the view was spectacular, sweeping over the fruit-trees, past the bamboo fence, over bleached stubble-fields, to a long sandy spit of beach at Parosporos to the south and to the u-shaped cove of Delfini to the north, both within five or ten minutes' walking distance. A perfect place to live.

"We can make a swing from this tree." Orla was already making arrangements for her amusement. "And Daddy can build us a house at the back of the garden where nobody will be able to see me and Fifi."

At one o'clock we were standing in Petros's shop, waiting for him to finish chopping up the carcass of a goat.

After he had locked the great, arched, medieval-looking door, Petros led us through yet another maze of streets to old Nomikos's house. We found the old man sipping his morning ouzo at the kitchen table. Nomikos was like a garden gnome, a tiny man with a handlebar moustache and devilish eyes looking out from under a cloth cap. Once again I cursed my lack of Greek. I dislike trying to communicate in grins and gestures. I feel at such a disadvantage, like a child among adults.

However, with the help of Petros, it did not take long to agree an annual rent. The only snag was that Nomikos, perhaps due to his advanced years and the uncertainty of his survival for twelve months, wanted all the money to be paid at once. We agreed; we would get the money somehow and, besides, he gave us a month in which to pay. To seal the deal, Rory and I had to join Nomikos and Petros in a round of ouzo and another of *raki*, a powerful local distillation not unlike poteen in its effect. Then, standing perilously on a chair, Nomikos took down an enormous iron key from a dusty shelf over his door and the little house at Parosporos, which we had decided to call Villa Ariadne, was ours. For the foreseeable future at any rate.

The Good Samaritan Wheelers collected all four of us and our bags from the room where we had been staying. We said goodbye to the generous old couple, Kyria Eleni and Kyrios Giorgos, packed their presents of fruit and vegetables into our rucksacks and set off like a gypsy caravan to our villa beside the sea. On an auspiciously sunny winter day our children and our goods were being transported on a mechanical plough by kind new friends to a wonderful house at the end of our rainbow. The plough and the stars, I thought, walking briskly behind, how

28

appropriate! We were to spend two of the most fulfilling and happy years of our lives in Villa Ariadne on the marble island of Paros.

It took a bit of juggling with the key before we could get the door open. Inside we found a hall, as large as a bedroom in many a suburban semi, warmly welcoming with its richly coloured and patterned tiles. At the far end of the hall, a back door opened onto a verandah from which stone steps led down to the garden. To the left of the hall was a large airy bedroom with two tall windows, one looking over the fields at the side of the house and the other onto a eucalyptus tree at the front. On the right was a living-room, the same size as the bedroom. Everything in this room, except the floor and walls, was brown. The square wooden table and the four chairs were toffee-coloured. The dresser in the corner was a chocolate brown and an island-style couch had a dark brown carved back and three mud-coloured lumpy cushions. As in the bedroom, two windows looked onto the front and side of the house. A door at the back of this room led into a small kitchen which had a stone sink set into the window embrasure and a fireplace, like a small cave, halfway up the wall, There was another brown wooden cupboard door and another exit to the verandah at the back of the house. A tiny, tacked-on room with a dry toilet was off the kitchen. There was no running water, no bathroom, no flush toilet or shower, but there was electricity. This, then, was our mansion. One bedroom for four people did not daunt us in the slightest. After all, we had been living in one room for months. And we would, no doubt, get used to living without running water or hot showers.

We dumped our rucksacks on the bedroom floor and

explored the garden. Then, having given a perfunctory dusting to the table, we laid out the bread, cheese, tomatoes, yoghurt and fruit we had brought with us from the village and ate the first of so many happy meals in Villa Ariadne.

We were woken very early on our first morning in our new home by a gentle tapping on our bedroom window. A vision from a Greek vase met my eyes when I opened the shutters to see who it was. Eleni was about fifteen years of age. Her long, black hair, curling in snaky ringlets to her waist, her slim nymph's figure, her large brown eyes and aquiline features would have inflamed the passion of Keats. She was leading a donkey whose creels were laden with vegetables. She was the youngest daughter of our neighbours, Elias and Maria, small farmers who were totally self-sufficient on their few hectares of land which adjoined our garden. We did not need to go very often to the village to shop after that. We bought eggs, fresh milk, goats' cheese, yoghurt, and all the fresh fruit and vegetables we could eat from Elias. We had the added bonus of daily deliveries made by a delightful creature on a donkey and the frequent gifts of figs, grapes or honeycombs, *yia ta paedia* (for the children).

A photograph taken during those first days on Paros shows the Brennan family standing outside the front door of Villa Ariadne on a warm afternoon in the glow of low winter sunlight. Rory, thin and wiry as a greyhound, his ribs poking like knobs through his yellow shirt, his broad forehead rising to light-brown, curly hair, his green eyes looking quizzically at the camera. Orla in her favourite dress, red gingham with a frill around the hem and a smocked yoke, sucking her thumb and smiling her shy, dissolving smile, her long, fair hair

30

flicking over her shoulders. Fiona, that little, tow-haired, round-faced, energetic being totally absorbed as usual by something outside the picture frame. I am still trailing remnants of what my friends call my "hippy days", the floating, flowery, Indian-cotton skirt, the embroidered top, the silver bracelets and the long, straight, red-brown hair. We look settled, contented, a family glad to be where we are.

There were a few things we needed to do to make Villa Ariadne a workable unit, with somewhere for all of us to be creative. The first thing we needed was a separate bedroom for the children, so that we could use our bedroom as a classroom for Orla by day, as a study for one of us in the evening and as a bedroom at night. The living-room would be a playroom on wet, cold days and would be transformed into a another study/studio for Rory or me in the evenings. We decided that the wide hall would make a perfect bedroom for the two girls. Rory devised a marvellous construction for their beds. He used bamboo poles we cut in the back garden to make a frame for bunk beds, strong enough for a five-year old and a toddler. We lashed rope, criss-cross, like an Indian charpoy, to make a base for the foam-rubber mattresses cut to fit in the village. I made a curtain and hung it from another bamboo pole halfway down the hall. We fixed one of those expandable wooden hangers to the wall, making a very cheap wardrobe, put their few toys into a cardboard box under the bunk beds, and Orla and Fiona had a bedroom of their own.

In the middle of the construction of the beds we had our first foreign visitor. Peter was a Canadian in his mid-twenties who had made lots of money working on oilfields in the frozen north. He lived alone in a rented farmhouse about a mile further up the valley. The Wheelers had told him a family had moved into the Parosporos house, so he called in to say *Hi* on his way to the post office. Observing the bamboo framework in the hall, he asked what we were making.

"Oh, it's just an altar to the household gods," replied my mischievous husband.

"The household gods? Gee! That's just great. Are they Celtic gods?" asked our visitor.

Chapter Three

Wind and Rain

When most people think of the Greek islands, images of infinite blue skies, a crystal-clear warm sea and sun-baked villages come to mind. Winter is different. As Lawrence Durrell says, "you must be young and fit to enjoy the necessary struggle against the rain and wind." When we arrived on Paros at the end of November the days still retained some of the summer warmth from about midday until three or four in the afternoon and it was still possible to swim for a short while on sunny days. After four, however, you needed a warm jacket or sweater.

On sun-blessed winter days in early December I often used to stand at a phone box at the OTE, the telephone office in Parikia, trying to get through to my family in far-off, troubled, grey Belfast. I would turn my back to the phone and look out over the bay as the ferryboat and the caiques came into the port and I would think, with a contented sigh, "This is real life. All that hustle and bustle, the constraints of the nine-to-five job, that rat-race, the traffic jams, the pollution, the drizzle and the grey, that's only half a life."

I would finally manage to get through the black hole that was the connection to Athens, through which all overseas calls were directed at that time and, when my mother would answer the phone, the chill of the dull, damp, industrial Northern streets would seep along the wires and into my bones. Shivering, I would turn again to look at the blue sea, the bright boats and the island of Syros on the horizon.

"Yes, everything's going fine here. The children love the island. The oranges and lemons are ripe in our garden and I spent yesterday making marmalade and lemon curd . . . The weather? Oh, it's just a perfect day. It'd lift your heart. What's the weather like there? . . . Cold, wet and windy . . . Ah well, spring will come along soon."

As the days went by, I was surprised to find that I missed very little about my previous busy life in Dublin. I didn't miss shops, theatres, or the excitement of city life. I didn't miss going out to work every day. I had loved my teaching jobs, I got on well with my colleagues and students, yet I missed none of them greatly. The only things I missed, apart from my family and friends, were birds, wild animals, tall trees and the local library. We did see the odd seagull over the bay but there were very few garden birds on Paros. Not enough food for them, I suppose, on a dry and rocky island. I never saw any wild animals, no rabbits or hares or hedgehogs, indeed nothing except rats and mice. As for trees, Paros has lots of fruit-trees, olive-trees and almond-trees, and there are eucalyptuses and some plane trees, but there is none of that abundance and variety of the beautiful tall trees I love so much in Ireland. A local library with English books would have been too much to hope for, so I would simply have to read the books I had brought with me slowly and swop books with any of the foreign community who enjoyed the same kind of books as I did. Still, there were many compensations. There were wonderful blessings in being at leisure on an island as beautiful as Paros. What do wealthy people long for? To be able to relax in a lovely place. What do so many people work for all year? To be able to afford a fortnight's holiday somewhere in the sun. And here we were, living in Greece in a lovely little villa by the sea, with plenty of leisure time to fulfil our creative needs and to enjoy our two daughters. I felt rich indeed, and blessed by the gods.

I had thought that, having gone out to work all my adult life, I might miss not only the salary, but the challenge, the sense of purpose, the company of colleagues, the feeling of belonging to the mainstream. But I did not feel unemployed, or that I was marooned in some backwater, out of the mainstream. No doubt, had I been living in the middle of Dublin, watching people I knew going to work, earning good salaries and living the comfortable bourgeois life, I might have felt differently. As it was, I was living among other "drop-outs", like the Wheelers, who were purposefully engaged in creative projects, who did not have much money either, so there was a reassuring equality of lifestyles and means.

Clouds! Grey skies over Parosporos! Not too long after we had begun to settle into Villa Ariadne, we woke one morning to a whole new landscape. By noon the entire valley was overcast with threatening clouds and the sea had turned the colour of gunmetal. Rain fell in piercingly cold arrows all afternoon and for the first time in months we could not go out. We realised then how little time we spent indoors. The children, confined to the house, were like frisky, tethered goats. They could not go out in the rain because, among all that excess baggage, their parents had not thought to pack useful things like raincoats, umbrellas or wellingtons. Our memories of Greece did not fit with grey skies and rain and we had foolishly disregarded our geography lessons about winter in continental climates.

There was a full laundry bag of dirty clothes in the bedroom and it was my turn to wash them. I peered through the rain at the well in the garden where we did the washing and decided that a shortage of clean towels was preferable to pneumonia. That night it was nose-bitingly cold and we shivered *en famille* in the wind-tunnel of the many draughts which whistled into the house from under the ill-fitting doors and moaned through gaps in the rattling window frames. We needed some source of heat, and soon.

Villa Ariadne had electricity, unlike the Wheelers' farmhouse. This was because it was on the main road and because old Nomikos, our landlord, who prided himself on being modern, had had electricity installed as soon it came to the island in the 60s. But there were no electric heaters for sale in the village. There were no heaters of any description for sale. So, using his ingenuity and some silver cigarette paper, Rory repaired a highly dangerous-looking contraption which a previous resident must have left behind. It was an Art Deco, circular electric fire with one bar which fizzled and sparked like a firework about to go off, but which threw out a weak heat if you sat right on top of it.

The weather grew colder daily and quite soon the heat from the eccentric electric fire was not enough even to take the chill off the air, never mind to keep us warm enough to read or for the children to play. Besides, the electricity supply was erratic and was often cut off for several hours a day, usually just as it became dark and colder, or when we were cooking dinner. We became obsessed with the need to keep warm, something we had rarely thought about in Hibernia!

Canadian Peter, our first foreign visitor to Villa Ariadne, was a kind fellow. Seeing how cold we were, he turned up one afternoon with a very welcome, if smelly, paraffin heater, which he claimed he did not need. Our daughters nicknamed him Peter Heater, and they loved him, not only for the heat, but for the great hunks of home-made bread and dollops of local honey he gave them any time we called to see him on one of our walks in the valley beyond Parosporos.

His gift kept us warm and happy for a few weeks until the supplies of paraffin ran out and no more could be found in any of the shops in Parikia or in any other village on the island. It could be weeks before new supplies would come, we were told. So we took to scouring the beaches at Parosporos and Delfini for driftwood and, when we had accumulated a damp pile of assorted planks and battered old fish-boxes, we lit a fire in the fireplace in the kitchen. The children gathered around excitedly, with their frozen little hands held up to the fire and expectations of warmth on their faces. Within minutes, clouds of choking smoke filled the kitchen and drove us, coughing and spluttering, into the drizzling garden.

Rory and I discovered, on climbing up onto the roof, that someone, probably Nomikos, had had a great slab of stone placed over the chimney, perhaps to prevent birds building their nests there. We heaved the great weight off the chimney. It was surely as heavy as the stone which the apostles had to drag away from the opening of the tomb of

Christ, but no miracle awaited us. The chimney continued to smoke so badly that we simply could not light a fire. There were no chimney-sweeps on Paros, so we never found out what the matter was.

"How do you keep warm?" we asked Elias and Maria when we went to pay our weekly bill. We communicated by means of gestures and grimaces, as we had not yet begun to get to grips with Greek.

"We live with the chickens," was their mimed reply.

Puzzled, we asked what they meant, as we knew that their chickens roosted in a ramshackle outhouse made of bamboo and old pallets.

"We get up at cockcrow and go to bed at sunset, like the chickens. During the day we're working hard and so we don't feel cold at all."

We did not want to live like chickens, however. The evenings, when the children were asleep, were precious, uninterrupted reading and writing time. We did not have the warmth-inducing agricultural work of our neighbours to keep us warm during the day and besides, small children feel the cold keenly. Our hunt for a source of heat continued. The weather became more Siberian every day. The rainfall increased to day-long drenching downpours and the north winds blew straight down from the Arctic and under our door. We took to wearing layers of clothes until we resembled the man in the Michelin tyre advertisement. We did not possess blankets for the beds; we could not afford to buy any in Parikia, and so had to make do with the sleeping bags we had brought in our rucksacks, supplemented with towels and anoraks piled on top for warmth. Some nights we slept like Inuit families in storybooks, parents and children all huddled up together for warmth.

38

Chapter Four

Deborah's Party

We had made Villa Ariadne as comfortable as we could, (if not as warm as we wished). The red and blue frame rucksacks were finally emptied and stacked behind the wardrobe and our books were arranged on shelves made from wave-planed planks found on the beach and hung by ropes from the ceiling beams. The bare light bulbs were shaded by lampshades made from wicker baskets hung upside down with their handles removed. The swing had been hung from the eucalyptus tree and a bamboo house had been built in the garden for the children. When we had established our marketing needs and strategy with Elias and Eleni, then we could lift our heads and look around us properly. We could begin to get to know the island and the other islanders.

Living in the countryside for the first time in my life, I became wonderfully aware of the richness of the natural world which was laid before me like a basketful of gifts. I wondered at the changing cosmos in the garden: the beginnings of the flowering of the almond-trees, the daily increasing cyclamen under the orange-trees and around the well, the landscapes of bark on the eucalyptus tree. I discerned for the first time the exact blue colour of the early-morning sky, like the Virgin Mary's mantle. I revelled in the unending theatre of the sea. Some days it played a hymn to peace, all gentle, dove-grey, glassy calm. And on stormy days scenes from *King Lear*, *Macbeth*, or *The Tempest* played on the stage at Parosporos. Witches' long grey hair, sky-big cloudy phantoms of dead kings, Caliban's foaming island.

And sounds too. Goat bells, very near, inquisitive outside our bedroom window, or mournful high on the hills above Agia Irini. Grunting mules snorting on misty mornings, clearing their noses. On Saints' Days, bells ringing from seldom-used small churches. And soft nocturnal scratchings of mice in the bamboo ceiling and behind the chocolate-brown cupboard in the kitchen. The screams of seabirds carried on the wind from far out at sea. The early morning clop-clopping of donkeys going laden to the market in Parikia, their lighter hoofsteps returning home in the evening. Thunder rolling in from Antiparos or Ios and from further around the Cycaldic ring of islands, bouncing off each island, its noise increasing like the crescendo of kettledrums in the finale of an orchestral concert.

And tastes. The incomparable crunchy taste of that-day-fresh organically-grown vegetables brought by our Grecian urn, Eleni, every morning. Creamy, nutty, grainy *tahini* spread on Maria's coarse bread. Liquid gold five-star Metaxa in Dinosaki's to warm you up on cold winter days before the walk back to Villa Ariadne with bags of shopping. The little bones of the *merides*, when the sea was calm enough for the caiques to go out and we could buy fresh fish. The tangy taste of *mizsitra*, Maria's goats' cheese, presented to us, *yia ta paedia*, in a blue ceramic bowl which was filled again as soon as we returned it, empty and washed.

And people. We had been on Paros for about two weeks before we met most of the rest of the foreign community who lived on the island. Shopping in the village one morning, we bumped into Clive and Phoebe in the bakery. They were chatting to another foreigner whom they introduced as Deborah. A striking-looking woman in her late twenties with long, dark hair in a thick, swinging ponytail, Deborah had the angular, faceted face of a Picasso portrait. She was a painter from Idaho who had been living on Paros for a couple of years.

"I'm a neighbour of yours," she told us. "I live about a mile further on, towards Agia Irini. You probably saw my house when you went to the Wheelers, it's right beside the road. Actually, I'm having a party tomorrow, why don't you guys come along and meet some more of us *xenia* on Paros?"

Deborah's party was typical of many of the parties we went to over the years on Paros. The guests were almost exclusively foreign residents. English was the lingua franca, the food and wine were Greek but the music, dancing and conversation were rarely Greek.

The people we met at Deborah's party were an interesting and varied group, the kind of multi-national group you might meet in a bar or at a party in Manhattan or London. There were two Dutch painters, several American writers, painters and photographers, some Germans who seemed to be engaged in building their own houses or houses for other people, an English woman

41

called Sheila who arrived in an ancient car with leather seats and a belching exhaust, an Italian woman called Marise who was married to an Australian bar owner in Naoussa and a French couple who had lived for years in Cairo. We learned that the all-year-round foreign community on Paros was about forty strong at that time and most of us were in our twenties or early thirties. Many of our fellow neo-Parians were artists of some sort. Most of them, like us, rented their houses. Mostly abandoned farmhouses, they said, with paraffin lamps and well-water, situated in picturesque but out-of-the-way places, up the sides of mountains, along rocky donkey-tracks or dried river-beds which were inaccessible to cars. These were places where few of the younger modern Greek islanders wished to live.

It seemed to me, because I like classifying, that there were four different categories of foreigners at that party.

First there were the artists, like Deborah and the Wheelers, who needed peace and quiet and a cheap place to live in a sunny climate where the landscape would provide stimulation and inspiration. Secondly there were the refugees who were fleeing from stressful jobs and lives in some European or North American city. Thirdly, there were the Lotus-eaters who simply wanted to live on the beach, drinking and eating, dancing and singing until their money or their visas ran out. Finally, there were the people connected with the art school in Parikia, the Aegean School of Fine Arts – resident teachers and the young American art students who came to attend courses at the school for a few terms.

Louisa and Annie did not easily fit into any of these categories. They were not full-time practising artists, although Annie wrote poetry when inspiration attacked her, and Louisa painted watercolours when she was not too busy doing other things. They were two intrepid American ladies who had left their grown-up children, their comfortable houses and lifestyles behind in New England and had come to live in island houses without any mod cons at all. Annie and Louisa, we were to find out, were a focal point of the foreign community. You never called on them in their different houses and found them alone. People visited them for their ever-ready coffee, their humorous advice, their witty company and their spellbinding stories.

Annie, who was the more comfortingly plump of the pair, wrote poetry as well as long philosophical letters to her scattered family of six children all over the United States. She lived in a house in the middle of the village in a maze of streets. You needed a trail of Hansel and Gretel's crumbs to find your way out again, if you managed to find your way there in the first place. But it was always worth getting briefly lost in the labyrinth. Annie had a subscription to *The New Yorker* and would pass on her copies when she had finished reading them. I never could get the jokes and wondered whether I was not clever enough to see the subtlety of the humour, but Annie assured me that you would need insider East-coast sensibilities to get the point.

Louisa, thinner and more physically active than her friend, lived in what Orla called the Geranium House, an ancient farmhouse up the rocky dried-up river-bed which made a path from Deborah's little house up to the mountain farms. Her artistry largely expressed itself in renovating other people's houses and in dreaming of finding her ideal house. She acted as an unofficial clerk of works. Whenever any of the foreigners needed help to

43

repair a leaking roof or to whitewash their house, Louisa would appear with a request to go to Lefkes or Pounda or somewhere else that had no precise name and had to be identified with complicated sketch maps, to help Claus or Ian or whoever to repair their roof or strip bamboos to make a new ceiling.

She was always on the look-out for a house to buy for herself and would walk all over the island searching out suitably dilapidated houses, stables or promising-looking heaps of rocks which she fondly imagined would not only be for sale, but would be also cheap enough for her to buy. Despite many disappointments, Louisa remained eternally optimistic that just around the next hill, or down that valley, her ideal house was waiting for her.

Perhaps because the rents were low, or they were not too concerned about the condition of these old houses, Parian landlords, Louisa warned me at the party, did not seem to consider that it was their responsibility to mend holes in roofs through which the rain poured in muddy streams in winter. Nor were they prepared to pay to have the houses whitewashed, or indeed to carry out any maintenance whatsoever. As the rents were low, however, most people did not object too much to having to do such work themselves. Nobody had much money, so they could not employ workmen, hence the need for a *meitheal*, as we call it in Ireland, a sort of a co-operative in which members of a community helped each other on a quid pro quo basis. At the end of a day's work repairing a roof or whatever, the happy householder would provide a big dinner and lots of farmers' wine for all the helping hands and another party was soon in full swing.

"Now, don't forget, if your roof leaks or you need any

help, just get in touch with me," Louisa said, "and I'll organise a work brigade."

Louisa went off to talk to Deborah about a problem with mice in her kitchen. A tall, thin man in his forties, with a nose like a parrot's beak, whose voice I had heard booming from the far end of the terrace, staggered over and introduced himself. "Hi, you're the new people in Judy's old house," he greeted us, in a drawling American accent, with a great thump on each of our shoulders. "Everyone calls me Doctor Dick. Glad to meet you."

We introduced ourselves and I tried to extricate my hand from his crab-like grip.

"Gee, so you guys are Irish! Great! I love the Irish, great little country you have there. The old Emerald Isle." He had the air of a restless vulture and was determined to impress us for some reason. He had got his doctorate in biochemistry at Trinity College, Dublin, he told us as if he had won a Nobel Prize. He went on to provide us with a convincing list and location of all the pubs in the vicinity of the university. He was originally Australian, he claimed, though he spoke with an American accent and had a British passport. He had lived all over the world, he told us, most recently in South Africa where he owned some fancy yacht which, he boasted, he had sailed up the east coast of Africa a few weeks before. He had abandoned it and the crew in what sounded like very mysterious circumstances.

"My daughter was born in Ireland. Westport. I'll show you her passport, you'll see." And he dragged out a battered passport from the inside of his Donegal tweed sports jacket. "The man doth protest too much," I thought. "What does it matter to us where his child was born?"

Doctor Dick became something of a pest. He would

turn up, usually fairly drunk, at Villa Ariadne at all hours of the day or night bearing gifts of chocolate for the children and waving a bottle of whiskey or cans of beer, thus making it quite impossible to turn him away. In such a small exposed house it was not easy to hide from anyone, so we were obliged to open the door. However, he did sing for his supper. Over the years we knew him, Doctor Dick's Walter Mitty adventures never failed to amuse us as we sat with straight faces listening to his impossible, drawling stories. He told us that he had worked in a hospital in the west of Ireland for a few years, but had been "run out of the country by the IRA."

"Why?" one of us asked.

"Because I was a double agent and the IRA found out. I was sure lucky. One of the local guys gave me a chance, gave me a warning in time, so I got my ass out of there quick."

"What do you mean, double agent?"

"I was recruited during my college days in the US by the CIA." (So he was educated also in the United States! Does the CIA recruit Australians?) "Once those guys get their hooks into you, you don't ever get to quit. I told them over and over that I didn't want to go on working for them, but they just kept on chasing my ass."

"And where did you go after you escaped from Ireland?"

"To Libya, to work for Ghaddafi."

Where else! Who else!

The exact nature of his work for the Libyan president was never, of course, made clear. Top secret. In fact, there was a lot about Doctor Dick that remained a secret. Eventually we believed nothing he said; his stories just did not make sense. Doctor Dick belonged in a category of his own, part Lotus-eater, part refugee, whole-time spinner of yarns.

His French wife had, according to Deborah, disappeared one day, a few months before our arrival. She simply never returned from a shopping trip to Parikia and left her two pale and undernourished-looking children to the untender mercies of their father. Throughout the winter months these poor waifs were frequently to be found wandering coatless along the road or standing at dusk on our or someone else's doorstep asking for food. A kindly retired Dutch couple, neighbours of "Doctor" Dick, often fed them and took them into their warm house from the cold. The children were like little mice; they scuttled around the place quietly, grateful for whatever little food they were given. They never talked about their mother and seemed to be in dread of their father.

As Doctor Dick was about to go into the house to get another plate of food, he was joined by a young woman who spoke to him about his children. He introduced her to us as Gloria, his children's tutor. Gold high-heeled shoes, tight leopard-skin trousers, a luminous pink jacket and matching lipstick, Gloria was glorious. I tried to fit her into one of my categories. She was not a Lotus-eater, if she worked for Doctor Dick. But why was she working for the man? I wondered. Perhaps she was a refugee. I looked forward to getting to know Gloria. I had to admire her style and her obvious determination not to succumb to the casual style of dress the rest of us had adopted. Although I felt quite dowdy, I wondered how she had negotiated the island roads in those high heels. Gloria sparkled like her name, and brought a whole welcome bagful of glamour to the island. The rest of us foreigners wore unisex jeans, sweaters, and sturdy boots in winter and T-shirts, shorts, and swimsuits in summer. We lived in rough places, in fairly primitive conditions and we dressed for comfort. I suspect some of us also wanted to get away from the compulsory business suits or dresses we had had to wear in our previous lives. Gloria's companions at the party were a kind young woman called Jeanne, who was, she whispered, Doctor Dick's rarely-paid housekeeper, and a happy-go-lucky Californian guy with a cheeky smile called Rob. Rob had driven down to Greece from Norway in a camper van and now ran an open house for homeless stray foreigners, Gloria said. We must come up there soon and meet the gang.

"Smiling Sue" was her nickname, a charming young woman with a wide smile and a diamond stud in her nose told me at Deborah's makeshift bar. She added that she lived in the Hilton.

"The Hilton!?" I asked. "I didn't know there was a hotel on the island."

"You know the shack beside the beach at Parosporos? "Well, we call that "the Hilton."

I put Sue into the Lotus-eater category, although she made her living as a part-time model at the life-drawing classes in the Aegean School and as an itinerant hairdresser. She was on the island to enjoy herself; she had spent a few years wandering around Europe and the Far East and Paros suited her perfectly right now.

Smiling Sue would cut your hair anywhere you chose, in your house, in "the Hilton" or, if it suited, at the beach. One day, we decided that Fiona's wispy baby hair needed a bit of shape put on it and hired Sue's services. She said she could do the job if we would bring Fiona the next morning to a vineyard on the outskirts of Parikia, which for some reason she was using as her outdoor salon at that time. Fiona, then aged three, sat on a tree-stump while Sue got out her scissors and comb.

"Could I see the style-book, please?" demanded her tiny client, who had seen Granny looking at such books in hairdressers' salons in Belfast. Fiona was most disappointed that this salon had neither a style-book nor a mirror in which she could monitor the haircutting progress.

Emily was, like Doctor Dick, in a category of her own, for different reasons – she was the only foreigner at the party who was married to a local Greek. She seemed to be a soft- hearted young woman with a great interest in the environment and in the esoteric.

Emily and her husband, Mikalis, lived in what I thought was one of the most beautifully located houses on Paros, right beside the beach at Parosporos. From her terrace you could hear the constant roar of the surf on windy days and watch the caiques going to fish off the shores of Antiparos. Emily passed our house almost every day on her bicycle on her way into Parikia and would often drop in to see if we needed anything in the village. Seeing me shivering beside the well, about to start washing the clothes one cold morning, she took the laundry bag from me and said she would put it in with her own and give it to her mother-in-law to wash in her washing machine.

Deborah's party was a turning-point in our early days on Paros. We met people with whom we became close friends and many others who helped us during our years on the island. And the friends we made at the party later introduced us to more people from other parts of the island.

Most of us foreigners had one thing in common, we came by most of our material needs in the same way, that is, second-hand. When somebody's children had grown out of their clothes or toys, they were passed on to the younger children in our community. Not so in the Greek community. There, it seemed, such communal wardrobes were not well regarded. I remember one occasion when I was sifting through a bundle of used children's clothes and toys in a large wicker basket on the floor of the shop of an American friend who ran a health-food business in Parikia, two Greek women came in and picked up some of the clothes.

"How much are these?" they asked.

"Oh, you can take them," replied my friend, "I'm just recycling them. People have given them to me for nothing, so if you like anything, please take it."

The Greek women were flabbergasted, "Oh, we couldn't do that. We thought they were for sale."

Adults, too, recycled clothes. We also passed on books, surplus pots and pans and other kitchen utensils. When somebody was leaving the island, they would hold a clearance party at which people could buy cheaply, or take away, the cushions, bedclothes, mattresses, odd pieces of furniture, gas rings, paraffin lamps, kitchen goods, books, audio-cassettes or whatever else the emigrants did not wish to transport back to America or wherever they came from or were going to.

Greece had not joined the European Union at that time and so foreigners were not allowed to work legally in the country. Many of the escapee foreigners on Paros who worked illegally, washing dishes or serving in bars and restaurants in the summer season, were ready to flee out the back door when the police raided the premises. Some supplemented their savings by doing housework or light construction work. One or two, who spoke fluent Greek and had good connections among the farmers, negotiated the sale of sites for rich Swiss and Germans who wanted to build summer villas on Paros. The artists sold their paintings, sculptures, photographs, jewellery, woven wall-hangings and ceramics to summer tourists. Many exhibited their finest pieces back home in New York or Munich in the winter months, thus making enough money to spend most of the year on Paros.

After Deborah's party, Rory and I had plenty of adult company, but we worried a little about companionship for our two daughters. Only a few of the foreign residents we had met so far had children and there were no Greek children living near us at Parosporos. However, after a month or so, we discovered that there were enough English-speaking children living on the island to keep Orla and Fiona company. As well as Emma and David Wheeler, there were half-a-dozen other children between two and six years of age. There was Hans, the six-year-old son of a Dutch-American couple, Victoria, the daughter of Marise the Italian and Robbie the Australian bar-owner in Naoussa. Then there was French Louis, whose parents, Michelle and Pierre, had spent years in Cairo.

One of our daughters' most regular playmates was five-year-old Phaedra, the polyglot daughter of our friends, Penelope and Jean-Pierre. Because her parents lived miles away on the other side of the island, Phaedra had to stay the night when she came to play. A solid little girl with a broad, untroubled face and long fair hair in plaits, Phaedra spoke Greek, English and French fluently and interchangeably. Our monoglot daughters were fascinated by the linguistic gymnastics of their friend and made up a language of their own to try to compete with Phaedra."

"What language are you speaking?" the puzzled child would ask.

"We're speaking Irish," Orla would reply. "Don't you understand it?"

Penelope and Jean-Pierre were not at Deborah's party. We were introduced to them in Naoussa by Marise. They were definitely in the artist category. He was an engraver and sculptor and she a talented weaver. They both spoke and wrote Greek fluently and did not mix with many of the *xenia*, living as they did in a very remote place and being more solitary by nature than most of the rest of us.

A tall, bearded Frenchman, Jean-Pierre walked for hours by himself all over the island, enjoying his own company and constantly on the look-out for any pieces of ancient pottery he could find. He had no time at all for small talk or island gossip. Within minutes of meeting him, you would find yourself discussing whether Picasso was all that he was cracked up to be or whether in fact he had copied many of his ideas from Juan Gris, not to mention Braque.

His wife, Penelope, was one of nature's free spirits. Born into a conservative, well-off family in Australia, she had spent her life rejecting those values and had lived a semi-nomadic, eccentric existence, just about managing to keep body and soul together by dint of selling her weaving, giving language lessons, accepting patronage where she could find it and generally making do with incredibly little money. Penelope was one of those mysterious people who had no visible means of support, yet managed to take off for six months to live in a Tibetan Buddhist monastery in Nepal or to travel around the coast of Australia. At this time, however, she had put down what, for her, amounted to a few roots on Paros. She had been living there with Jean-Pierre, her second husband, for five years by the time we arrived.

The last category of foreigners was the Aegean School of Fine Art gang. We met the founder of the school, Bert

Edwards, a tall, thin, charismatic American, at that famous party and took the earliest opportunity to go and visit him at the school in Parikia. The art school is still located in several buildings around Parikia. The main centre is a tall, unsteady-looking Venetian mansion in the middle of the village. It has wonderful, high, airy rooms with shaky wrought-iron balconies. The toilet is in a tiny room that hangs off the side of the building like an ageing limpet whose clinging powers are waning. It looks quite capable of letting one go in mid-stream, as it were. At the end of the seventies the school employed about six or seven foreign artists as teachers of painting, sculpture, ceramics, photography, print-making, and creative writing. Bert's idea for his school was that students would come to the island, live with the local people, be inspired by the landscape and culture of a beautiful Greek island, and the end result would be art. Most of the students at the school were from North America and came for a semester or two for which they could gain credits at their colleges in the States.

Bert had five great loves: his partner Christine, the Aegean School, his saxophone, his glass of wine, and telling stories. He and Christine lived in a extremely run-down, but very tidy rambling farmhouse outside the village. Their long-term house guest was a rather testy kestrel which had injured one of its wings and which inhabited the living-room. The house was always full of his Greek neighbours or students who came with problems or who were a bit homesick. Bert entertained the students with his stories and music. He arranged visits to *panagyris* (festivals) in monasteries in the countryside. He rented rooms for his students in ancient village houses. He got deals for them with barbers, greengrocers, and tavernas. He captured passing musicians and poets to give concerts and readings at the school. And every year he organised a traditional Greek Easter party with dyed crimson eggs and roast lambs on a spit.

Over the years there were quite a few students at the Aegean School who did not go back to the States when the art course was over but stayed on Paros for a while to work as artists or later on to teach at the school. One of the students who never returned, a guy from Texas who made mixed-media pieces from driftwood and fishing-weights, became a fisherman. He joined the crew of local caiques and spent weeks at a time fishing around the shores of Paros and of other islands. Two of the female students we met, Diana and Monica, fell in love with and married Greeks.

Student exhibitions at the School were highlights of the local social scene, an excuse for a party and an opportunity to exchange gossip. Our gossip was not usually malicious, it mainly consisted of who was coming and going from the island.

At one of the student exhibitions we met Grace, the oldest student to attend the Aegean School. A tiny, smartly-dressed, silver-haired, American widow, she seemed very pleased to meet a young family and she invited us to her house for afternoon tea. There she told us how she had come to Paros and why she had stayed. Six months before, her beloved husband had died at home in Los Angeles. She was over sixty, her three children were grown up, married and living elsewhere. Grace considered her future. She did not relish a life of sedate coffee mornings and lunches in the plush suburb where she had brought up her children. Shortly afterwards she saw an advertisement for the Aegean School in a magazine, booked her place and arrived on Paros with a bundle of paintbrushes and a determination to enjoy herself. Grace learned to paint delicate, light-filled watercolours, which she exhibited in restaurants in the village as well as at the Aegean School shows. When the art course finished, she could not bring herself to leave the island, so she bought a two-roomed house, just big enough for a tiny person like herself, which overlooked an unexpected orchard in the middle of the village. There she dispensed coffee, cognac and sympathy to all of us who dropped in to see her. Orla and Fiona adored her. She replaced their grandmothers in a way, and she had the added fascination of having gone to school with Marilyn Munro. Grace had a natural talent for mixing with young people. Old enough to be our mother, she was ageless. Her good-humoured, positive outlook on life endeared her to everyone and she was automatically included in all our parties and outings. Grace was a natural islander, with an ability to fit in anywhere and to get on with those among whom she found herself.

Stefan, too, was a natural islander, part Lotus-eater, part artist. Born in South America of German parents, he was a tall, handsome and powerfully-built young man in his early twenties when we met him on a stormy day in our salon, Dinosaki's kafeneion. He came in through the door in a burst of raw energy and bonhomie, accompanied by his bride, Claudia, a tiny, small-boned woman of Vietnamese origin, who had been brought up in Brazil and France. He looked like a Viking god, as tall and blonde as she was tiny and dark. Stefan was the son of artistic parents, a painter and a film director. He had had a nomadic childhood and spoke at least four languages fluently. He spoke English to us, Portuguese and French to Claudia, and German to his parents and their German friends. His parents had built a wonderful house on Paros and had finally settled there, so

Stefan had brought his bride to stay for a while with his family. He had a dare-devil air about him. He could swim further, dive deeper, catch more octopus than anyone else. He seemed to whirl around the island in a gale of energy, even though his only means of transport was a second-hand 50 cc moped.

One of my lasting memories of Stefan was at dusk one February evening. We were, all four of us, riding our little blue Honda moped on our way to a *Mardi Gras* party in Judy the Painter's house. Rory, the children and I were all disguised, with varying degrees of success, in fancy dress. As we bumped along the dirt road, tiny Fiona perched on the front of the bike, tied on to her father, Orla sandwiched between us and myself forming the final wedge, we were overtaken in a cloud of dust by a figure on another motor-bike. A great, black, voluminous cloak billowed out behind the rider. A tall top hat covered half his eye and an enormous fanged tooth protruded over his lip and gleamed a ghostly white in the fading light. Stefan as Count Dracula on his way to the party.

Many of the foreign residents on Paros had interesting stories to tell, how and where they had lived BP (Before Paros), as I call it, how they had landed up on this island, why they stayed on. Everyone had time to talk. Here you took people at face value. Who or what they were BP did not matter. All you saw and heard the person sitting at your cafe table sharing an ouzo or cognac with you. There was a tremendous liberation in that. An equality, it seemed to me, that was not possible in the other world from where we all needed to escape for a time, for one reason or another.

Chapter Five

Winter Festivities and Occupations

Back home in Ireland we were used to large family gatherings and parties at Christmas, so the prospect of a nuclear family Christmas on Paros was distinctly unattractive. We had to have a Christmas party in Villa Ariadne. We would serve mulled wine with Christmas pudding and cake. Even if we had found turkeys for sale on Paros, we had nothing to cook one on or in.

That year I made the first Christmas pudding of my life, my mother or mother-in-law having always obliged in the past. I then set about solving the problem of the cake. Without an oven, this was something of a challenge. But I knew of someone who had an oven. Elsa, a German woman, who always looked to me like a First World War spy in her leather flying-jacket and helmet sitting astride her powerful, bright-yellow motor-bike, agreed to let me use her gas oven to bake my cake. She collected me at Villa Ariadne two days before Christmas and I climbed onto the pillion seat of her motor-bike with all the ingredients for my cake in a wicker basket. Elsa was one of the few foreigners at that time who owned her own house. It was a beautiful old farmhouse, with a dovecote and enormous bread-oven, set among olive-trees and vines. The house was near the famous Valley of the Butterflies, much frequented by summer tourists who come to shake the trees and watch the clouds of brilliant crimson-winged butterflies darken the air. Her Greek was fluent and she made her living partly by locating sites and houses for rich Germans and Swiss people who wanted to own a place on Paros. Some people resented this. They believed that by bidding for land and houses for rich clients, most of whom would only come for a few weeks in the summer, she was putting up the prices of houses for Greeks to rent or buy, as well as making it more expensive for the rest of us, who wanted to live full-time on the island.

A determined woman who brooked no indecision, Elsa demanded on arrival at the farmhouse, "It vill take some hours for zis cake to bake, so vhich music you will listen to while ve vait?"

"If you have anything by Haydn, that'll suit me fine," I replied. I could see by her expression that I had passed some sort of test, that if I had said, "Oh, anything you like," I would not have merited further acquaintance and might have had to come away with a half-baked cake.

Christmas morning was numbingly cold and very windy. The orange and lemon-trees were battered by the storm and scattered their fruit in a golden carpet in the garden. Santa Claus was not rich that year. She brought a hand-knitted hat and scarf for each of the girls, a book each and some packets of sweets. At midday our guests began to arrive on foot, by motor-bike, on donkey, and a few by taxi.

We had invited all the foreigners we knew on the island as well as Elias, Maria, Eleni, Nick Hamburger, Evangelis, the clerk from the bank, and our landlord, Nomikos, who arrived with presents for our children: two tins of hairspray and a bar of chocolate each. Another guest was Andreas, a new neighbour who had arrived from Athens to work on the radio station on Mount Profitas Elias. He had rented the building across from Villa Ariadne which until then we had thought was some kind of warehouse. He brought his Irish girlfriend, Sarah, who had come to Greece on a fortnight's holiday, met Andreas and stayed on to live with him.

Christmas is not at all as important a feast in Greece as it is in Ireland. There was none of the festive air in the village or in people's houses which the children associated with the season. So we had made our house look as Christmassy as possible with the "tree" – a few pine branches decorated with balloons. We lit candles and strung paper chains across the living-room.

Of course, no sooner had everyone arrived than there was an electricity cut which went on for hours. The Polish workers at the power station, no doubt, were drinking their Christmas vodka and having their own party. We had to rely on body heat and many jugs of mulled wine to keep our guests warm. We heated the mulled wind over a battery of candles. Nick Hamburger, a Greek-American from Chicago who owned the first hamburger joint on Paros, had brought along photocopies of Christmas carols for us all to sing. The resulting concert was a hilarious cacophony as the English, American, Dutch, French, Irish and German versions of the tune differed as much as the words of the different carols. Finally, we sang in language groups, which was moderately more successful. Our Greek guests taught us some island dances, which had the double advantage of keeping us warm and on the floor. With only four chairs and the couch in the living-room, we did not have enough seating for everyone, so dancing in turns was encouraged while the seated ones ate slices of pudding and cake and drank quantities of mulled wine from every vessel in the house, including the tooth mug.

Orla, Fiona and Phaedra went missing for a time and were discovered with chattering teeth and blue nose-tips in the bamboo play-house in the garden "tasting" the mulled wine and the Christmas cake they had filched from the kitchen. They had to be thawed out for half-an-hour with hot chocolate drinks and hot-water bottles.

On St Stephen's night the roof leaked for the first time, like a colander. We were woken by cries from the girls who came running into our bedroom in sodden pyjamas. Within minutes the torrential rain had penetrated our bedroom ceiling as well and drenched our bed. There was no point in moving the bed to another part of the room because the entire roof was like a sieve. The electricity was off again, but we could hear the raindrops pattering all over the tiled floor. We foraged for candles in the dark kitchen and provided a temporary solution to leaks on the bed by spreading large, black, plastic refuse sacks over the bedclothes. Not giving a hoot about bad luck, we put up two recently purchased umbrellas. The Brennan family then spent the rest of the night huddled in one bed, while raindrops splattered on the umbrellas and rat-tatted on the plastic bags.

Wet bedclothes and mattresses in a house without heating and with a leaky roof in a wet climate does not make for a healthy environment, so the *meitheal* had to go into action on our behalf. Word went out, via Louisa, that the roof of Villa Ariadne was leaking badly. A few hours later the gang appeared with ladders, cement and some sticky, black, tar substance to plaster over the cracks in the roof. The rain had mercifully stopped and the job was done in two hours.

Traditional Parian roofs are made by resting large wooden beams, usually chestnut, across the walls. Stripped bamboo canes are then tied on over the beams. Next comes a layer of seaweed as insulation and finally layers of alluvial clay which bakes as hard as cement in the summer sun and is impermeable for a year or so until cracks appear and more clay has to be added, making roof maintenance an annual chore.

When we went into the village the following day to tell Nomikos about our leaks, he appeared cheerfully indifferent to our sodden tale of woe. The very same had happened to him, he told us. "No problem," he said. "Easy to fix. Would you like me to tell you how I deal with leaks?" He demonstrated his solution by taking off his boots and getting into bed wearing his overcoat and cap and recommended that we do the same. "*Kala*," (good) he said, beaming, and drank another glass of ouzo.

On the eve of 6th January, the feast of the Epiphany, there was a *panagyri* in the old Byzantine monastery of Taxiarchis, which is on a hill halfway between Parikia and Naoussa. The monastery, like so many in Greece, had been virtually abandoned since the fall-off in vocations to the clergy left these lovely places without monks. Taxiarchis belonged to the few remaining old monks in the nearby monastery of Longevarde, who make their living by painting icons on wood in the traditional manner. On festival days, some of the Longevarde monks came over to Taxiarchis to celebrate the service. Our friends, Penelope and Jean-Pierre, lived near Taxiarchis and invited us to come to dinner and then to attend the *panagyri* with them early the following morning. Our hosts' house was a very simple farmhouse built in traditional island style whereby one room was built at a time and the others added on as the family grew, or money was available. The original room was a low, cube-shaped structure with a bread-oven in one corner. Along the back wall there was a stone-built structure about four feet high and six feet long which had a dual function. The stone structure was covered by a wooden hinged lid on top of which a flock mattress was laid. It was a grain-store-cum-double-bed. Cheeses, vegetables and loaves of bread were protected from mice and ants by being hung in baskets suspended from a ceiling beam. In this one room a young married couple would have lived, cooked, and slept. In time, two other rooms, the children's bedrooms, would have been added on. Doors to all three rooms led off an open courtyard. There were no interconnecting internal doors so you had to go into the cold courtyard in winter in order to get to the toilet or to bed. There was no bathroom and the toilet was a wooden seat over a hole in the ground located in a small dry-stone hut behind the house. The house had no electricity, but at least the paraffin lamps provided a modicum of heat as well as light.

Penelope usually cooked on a gas cooker fuelled by a gas-cylinder, but the gas had run out and she had to make do with burning driftwood in the bread-oven. The island suffered from frequent gas-cylinder as well as paraffin shortages and electricity blackouts. As there had been gale-force winds for almost a week, no new gas-bottles could be brought in. Adults and children sat huddled around the dinner table in the kitchen wearing our coats, hats, scarves and gloves. Had Vincent Van Gogh been passing he could have used us as latter-day models for his early painting, *The Potato Eaters*, so miserable did we look in the sickly yellow light of the paraffin lamps. So Arctic was the temperature in the room that, when dinner was finally served, our hands were too cold to manipulate the knives and forks and we had to take it in turns to go to the bread-oven and thaw out our frozen fingers sufficiently to be able to eat. It is not easy to carry on a dinner-party conversation when one's toes are like lumps of ice and one's breath hangs in the frosty air like a cumulus cloud.

Our hosts and their little daughter, Phaedra, slept all together for warmth in the grain-store bed while we four squashed into one cramped and damp bed in the bedroom across the courtyard in the hope that our combined body heat would save us from hypothermia. We did not have to be wakened before dawn to get ready for the *panagyri*.

It was still dark as we picked our way up the steep, stony path to the monastery. Islanders on donkeys or mules and on foot passed us shouting *Kronia pola* (Many years), to which we replied, *Episis* (And the same to you). Inside the ancient vaulted church, stout, hand-made beeswax candles spluttered in icy draughts and ancient bearded monks who looked like the saints in their own painted icons, intoned endlessly, interrupting themselves to kiss the images of the Virgin and of the saints. The local farmers and their families made up the congregation. As they blessed themselves and prayed, their shadows cast grotesque, giant shapes on the rough, whitewashed walls of the monastery. Beyond the walls we could occasionally hear the braying and restless chomping of their donkeys and mules, tethered to the centuries-old plane tree in the courtyard. It was a scene out of a medieval painting.

Fiona lay across my lap, clasping her teddy and sucking a quietening lollipop while the other two girls amused themselves by solemnly lighting candles and imitating the congregation with many signs of the cross and much thumping of their breastbones.

During the cold, windy months between December and March we found heat and company in Dinosaki's kafeneion. During these winter months, shopping trips became a social occasion for us foreigners. We were drawn like moths to the lamp of Dinosaki's. We met there at mid-morning after we had finished our shopping to drink cognac and Greek coffee and to eat Dinosaki's famous *mezedes*, which are the little titbits traditionally served with ouzo. His well-stocked pot-bellied stove threw out miraculous heat. We pulled our chairs in a circle around it and we gossiped, read our mail, made arrangements for children to come to play with each other, exchanged valuable information about the possible location of elusive gas-cylinders and supplies of paraffin, recycled clothes, swopped paperbacks and old newspapers from home, and organised parties.

Our parties were frequent, effortless and communal. Everyone brought food and litres of farmers' wine in wicker-covered glass demijohns. We often brought sleeping bags and blankets because many parties were all-night affairs in remote houses up difficult tracks. Too difficult to negotiate in the dark after an evening of *retsina* and *mavro* – dark red Parian wine.

The children came everywhere with us. Even if there had been available babysitters, we could not have afforded to pay them much or as often as we went to parties. In any case, children were regarded as part of life on Paros. They came with their parents to kafeneions and tavernas and fell asleep at the table when they tired of running around playing in the safe streets.

On our way to and from the winter-time parties we would examine the newly rain-washed stone walls and tracks for shards of pottery and other interesting objects which were often flushed out by the rain. Thus we gradually gathered a treasure trove: ceramic loom-weights, bits of broken pots, some from as far back as the geometric period, pestles, and handles of *amphora*. "Pottry!" the children would shriek at every glimpse of a terracotta shape among the rocks at the base of dry-stone walls.

Much later, when we showed our collection of broken pieces to the archaeologist in charge of the Cyclades, she took some pieces away to be photographed in the museum before returning them to us. But we never found the greatest prize of all, one of the marble Cycladic idols, wonderfully enigmatic modernistic sculptures of which there are many examples in the British Museum. Of course, had we found anything like that we would have handed it into the museum in Parikia. I am sure we would.

Living in a house without a bathroom or running water, where clothes had to be washed in cold water by a well, where children had to be bathed in the kitchen in a large tin tub filled with relays of kettles of hot water meant that a lot of our time was spent on labour-intensive activities. Add to this, the time required to walk the mile or so into the village to buy and carry home groceries. A good deal of time was also required to educate Orla who had already spent one year at school in Ireland and who could read and write quite well. Rory and I could both have been kept busy enough all day long, and the whole objective of our sojourn in Greece could have been subverted in domestic business and busyness.

Our solution was to divide the week into OFF and ON days. On Mondays, Wednesdays and Fridays, for example, I would be OFF. I could choose to make pots, continue my spinning lessons with Maria next door, go walking in the mountains with a friend or, if I chose to, stay in bed all day and stare at the ceiling. Rory would be ON those days and was responsible for the complete running of the house as well as the care and entertainment of the children. If one of them fell out of a tree, he would bandage and kiss better. He would teach Orla in the mornings, do the shopping, wash the clothes and do whatever else needed doing. On Tuesdays, Thursdays and Saturdays the roles were reversed. Sunday was a family day with both parents on duty. Thus we both had time to do the things we had come to the island to do.

And we could boast of some achievements during our first winter on Paros, the results of time well-spent. Rory spent the dark months writing a collection of poetry which he sent off to a publisher in Ireland. Not only did the publisher agree to publish it, but it won a major literary prize, which encouraged him to continue writing poetry. He has done so ever since. He read voraciously as usual, history and biographies, as well as poetry and novels.

My own pursuits were more hands-on. I had decided that I needed to do something with my hands as well as with my brain. I learned how to spin and weave. I bought fleece from Elias's brown and black sheep which I washed in the sea. Maria taught me how to card the tangled wool and prepare it for spinning. We bought a drop spindle in the village, the kind you see nomadic women in bright costumes using in *The National Geographic* magazine; the kind of spindle, no doubt, that was used to spin the wool for Joseph's coat of many colours.

The spinning lessons took place in the lull of the afternoons in Maria's kitchen. I would spend hours trying not to look stupid as the thread broke once again and the spindle crashed to the floor. Maria would tut-tut and pick it up. "It's easy," she said, "a child can do it. Look, just hold it like this and concentrate. No, no, you're getting great lumps in the wool. It should be all the same thickness. Look at mine. If it's all lumpy like yours, how can you weave or knit with it?"

Finally I got the hang of it. Like drawing and painting, spinning demands that you are calm and concentrated. It's a bit like Zen meditation, the harder you try the less successful it is. When I was centred, my wool spun even and strong. If I was any way agitated, the thread was uneven and lumpy. Maria did not weave, she used her wool for knitting sweaters and for crocheting bedcovers. So Penelope offered to teach me how to weave if Rory would make me a simple frame loom. He obliged, and Penelope and I spent hours on the back porch in the weak winter sun setting up the loom and starting the weaving project. When I had mastered the frame loom and had made a few wall hangings, Penelope said she would let me use her big floor loom.

She had a whole room in her house devoted to weaving. The loom took up most of the space and cones of wool brightened the shelves around the walls. Penelope made waistcoats to sell in the shops in Parikia and Naoussa. She also made enormous wall hangings in earth colours from wool she carded and spun herself. She hoped to sell these in Athens, or in a friend's gallery in Amsterdam.

I loved the rhythm of the flying shuttle, the satisfying

thump of the wooden bar you use to bang the weaving into place after every line. Hours passed without my noticing and it was only when I could hardly see any more in the darkness that I realised I had spent all afternoon and evening at the loom without lifting my head or thinking about anything except the growing length of woollen material in front of me. Weaving is a marvellous way to forget your troubles. The result of my industry was a heavy waistcoat in black, brown and white wool, a bit like one a Greek shepherd in Epirus might have worn at the beginning of the century – a present for Rory. He wore it once to a party and the ungrateful fellow sheepishly took it off after half an hour, saying that he was going to die of heat and that he felt as if he was wearing a carpet on his back.

Not content with spinning and weaving, I wanted to learn how to use natural dyes on my wool. So I collected onion skins, the shells of walnuts, lichen from rocks and anything else I thought would produce a good colour. Our little kitchen was filled with steaming pots of different brews which I used for my dyes and the garden line dripped with hanks of wet wool. I ended up with motley skeins of wool in unappealing shades of brown, black, and yellow with some weak greens and light oranges. I can really appreciate the depth and variety of colours those nomadic tribes in Turkestan or Baluchistan achieve from vegetable dyes for their wonderful carpets.

I wrote a lot of desperately serious short stories that winter in blue, plastic-covered exercise books. I learned new tunes on the tin whistle and realised ruefully that enthusiasm does not compensate for lack of talent. So, when I played the whistle in the garden on sunny days, where hopefully nobody could hear me, I did not fool myself that, with practice, I could be a female James Galway.

Rory and I both enjoyed being close to nature. We knew the phase of the moon without having to look out the window at night. We did not need to listen to weather forecasts because we began to learn the signs of the sky and the sea. Very specially, we were able to spend more time with our young children than most parents can afford. They were not so much young human beings to be clothed, fed and looked after, as an inseparable part of our lives – rather like the children I had seen on their mothers' backs in the fields or around the cooking-pots in the villages of Zambia where I once worked for a year.

Our division of labour, however, was not very popular with our new neighbour, Andreas. One morning he came over to ask Rory something, to find the "poor man" teaching Orla to read while bandaging the knee of Fiona who had once again fallen off the swing on the eucalyptus tree. The smell of lunch cooking wafted from the kitchen and the laundry was steeping in a tin bath. Meanwhile I was sitting at the table reading. He went home and told his girlfriend that she was to have nothing to do with me as I had somehow bewitched my poor husband into doing all the work while I, the woman of the house, the wife and mother, sat around with my head in a book. She explained that the following day the roles would be reversed, but he shook his head and said that such work was always woman's work and that no Greek man with self-respect would allow such a thing.

On Sundays we took the children on long exploratory walks. We combed the beaches for driftwood for the fire, or for washed-up fish-boxes which we could make into book-cases or shelves for the kitchen. Occasionally, especially if there was a *panagyri*, we went to the beautiful, fourth-century Byzantine basilica, the Ekatonpyliani, in Parikia. We loved the ritual, the colour, and the ceremony, the *Kyrie elision* chanting of the bearded pony-tailed priests, the rich silver-encrusted icons, the candlelight flickering on the frescoed domes, the whole inclusive atmosphere where people came and went, lit candles, lifted children up to kiss icons and gossiped with their neighbours against the stage set of one of the most magnificent churches in all of the Greek islands.

Ekatonpyliani (meaning either the "Church of the One Hundred Doors" or alternatively "The Church Below the Town") is said to have been built on the instructions of St Helena, she of the relics of the true cross and mother of Constantine the Great. The saint was forced by gales to land on Paros on her way to the Holy Land. Legend has it that she vowed to build a church on the island if she arrived safely in Constantinople. Although there is evidence that the construction started in the fourth century, the main work was carried out in the fifth century when Justinian sent his architect, Isodore, and others who had built St Sophia's in Constantinople, to Paros.

I love the atmosphere in Byzantine churches. For they are glowingly dark and mysterious places. Places which appeal to all the senses: the rich coloured wall-paintings, the hundreds of beeswax candles, the chanting priests, the cool silver-covered icons which the worshippers kiss, the fat loaves of bread which you are given to eat on special occasions. They are like what the crowded Gothic cathedrals must have been like in the thirteenth century.

I also like being in buildings which are built on top of something else. It is like participating in the layers of art history, standing on the top stratum. Wondering what new structure will be built there when you are long dead. The Ekatonpyliani was built on the foundations of a third-century Roman gymnasium or school for athletes. So, when you are lighting a candle in front of the icon of the Virgin, you can imagine the shouts of the victorious athletes and the buzzing of the spectators on prize-giving sports' days. The columns in the basilica came from a Doric temple built in the sixth-century BC. When you lean against these marble wonders you can glimpse, just around the other side of the column, a worshipper of Diana in a flowing white robe tied at the waist with a girdle.

The Ekatonpyliani was finished in the sixth century AD. More layers were laid on top of the basilica throughout the centuries as each generation wanted to modernise their church, so that by 1959, when an extensive restoration project was started, the Byzantine character of the church had largely disappeared and had to be restored.

Every year on the 15th August, the feast of the Assumption of the Virgin Mary into heaven, the basilica is the focus of a great *panagyri* which rivals the celebrations on the island of Tinos. Pilgrims come to Paros from all over Greece and many sleep overnight in the aisles and courtyard while the ceremony goes on, amid incense and chanting, until the early hours of the morning. The famous icon of the Virgin is carried in procession through the streets and is showered with rose petals from balconies and windows along the route.

Another of my planned winter occupations was the study of philosophy. Living on such ancient soil with its many layers of different civilisations, its happy mix of relics from the ancient Greek, the Roman, the Byzantine and

71

Venetian epochs, this would indeed be the place, I was sure, where the words of Socrates and Plato *et al* would be easy to understand.

I had brought as many philosophy books as I could carry in my rucksack but my course-reading material was by no means complete. I needed Heidegger, Wittgenstein, and Popper, to name a few. My mother kindly posted some books to me and I was very lucky to find Sheila, the young English woman from Deborah's party with the leather-seated car, fresh out of university with a degree in philosophy and now washing dishes illegally in Parikia. She had brought many of her philosophy books with her and was most willing to lend these to me and to indulge me in philosophical discussions, which frequently took place by candlelight in gloomy dark stable she rented as a house.

Another factor which I found made the study of philosophy easier and more enjoyable on Paros was the quiet, simple lives we were leading. We had no distractions from newspapers, television or video. I lived closer to nature than at any other time in my life, apart from my first year in Africa. Stripped to the essentials, conscious of the smells and rhythms of nature, I found philosophy, which asks the most fundamental questions, more meaningful and less academic than when read in university libraries in noisy, polluted, distracted cities.

We were not totally cut off from the outside world. We listened to the World Service of the BBC, but as we could only get a clear reception at certain times of the day, our listening was limited. We heard enough to know what was going on in the world. We were well enough informed about the negative events: plane crashes, earthquakes, crop failures, and conflicts everywhere, the depressing terrorist acts in Italy, the endless war in the

Middle East, the senseless violence in the north of our own country.

I, who had been so politically involved for years, as well as belonging to many pressure groups from Amnesty International to CND to local issue groups, found myself strangely detached from it all. Not unconcerned, not uninterested, just on a different wavelength. I think that when one is living in a city, bombarded with horrific images on television screens, as well as by headlines and photographs in daily newspapers, the impact of the evil and unnecessary misery in the world is much more acute than when one hears the same news on the radio in a high-ceilinged room looking out over a blossoming orange-grove to the waves breaking on a golden beach on a beautiful, small Aegean island.

Is it the case I wonder, that one of the results of too much exposure to visual horror is that many people simply turn off? So many people read "newspapers" containing no news at all, just endless seedy stories about vicars and tarts and the vainglorious corruption of politicians, with no analysis and no difficult questions asked. The soaps, the glamour movies and the thrillers, watched by millions of people all over world, may be an antidote to a surfeit of real horror, a mental survival tactic.

On my little island I began to feel that I was becoming a bit like one of those detached Buddhist monks I had met some years before in Nepal, near the Tibetan border, knowing something about the conflict, the misery and the suffering that was going on in the world, not uncaring, but determined to get on with their own lives of prayer and meditation and, in that way, to recompense for the evil, to balance the scales. Of course, I was not foolish or arrogant enough to think of myself as enlightened. I was not living a monkish life. My days were not devoted entirely to spiritual devotion. I was, and still am, attached to far too many things of this world. Nonetheless, living simply, with very few material possessions, with time to reflect, to meditate, to refresh my mind, to observe the daily changes in the physical world around me, to play with my children, I felt cleansed. I believed that I was in touch with something beyond the never-ending conflict to which we humans seem to be addicted; something more holistic which did not ignore the reality and pain of conflict, but which allowed me to pay attention to the small things in the here and now, to the tiny daily springs of hope and renewal. I felt both connected and detached. That is the paradox. I was learning. Life lessons.

Chapter Six

Lessons to Learn

One of our main winter occupations was teaching our daughter, Orla. She had started primary school just after her fourth birthday so she had already spent a year in junior infants and could already read and write quite well and had a reasonably good vocabulary in both English and Irish. We were not concerned that our daughter would miss out on schooling while we lived in Greece. After all, we were both teachers and besides, at that age, she would not miss too much. Nonetheless, we had bought all the books she would have been using in school had we stayed in Dublin and we determined to teach her ourselves at home.

The experience of trying to teach Orla has convinced me that parents should never, ever, attempt to teach their own children. No matter that they are professional teachers, with the best intentions in the world, no matter that they may have read all the educational psychology texts, it simply is not a good idea. I prided myself on being very patient with students, no matter what their learning problems. I thought I was a tolerant, encouraging and kind teacher. I found out, very quickly and to my great dismay, that my patience and tolerance did not extend to my own child, that I was, at times, extremely intolerant, irritable and unfair. When the poor child failed to grasp something or forgot something I thought I had taught her the day before, it was as if my own intelligence was under question. After all she was my daughter, she had my genes and now she could not understand or remember this simple thing!

I would go into the "classroom" full of good intentions and zeal. Within half an hour I had reduced myself to a screaming harridan.

"But Orla, what do you mean, you never heard of that? We spent ages learning it two days ago, and Daddy did it again with you yesterday."

The poor child was reduced to a nervous wreck who could hardly remember her own name by the end of the "lesson". It was not always like that, of course, but such scenes happened too often and I was ashamed of my behaviour and only slightly consoled by the fact that Rory had similar experiences and felt equally frustrated and annoyed with himself. Orla, a most tolerant and kind girl, does not, however, seem to hold our bad teaching against us. English and Irish reading, spelling and writing, arithmetic, art and crafts, drama, physical education, nature study, we all three valiantly struggled through these subjects, some a lot more easily than others. Orla is naturally gifted in art and needed little teaching, all she required was enough materials and encouragement. She loved reading too, but found arithmetic difficult. She was not greatly helped to master number concepts by the fact that maths is not the forte of either of her parents.

However, we completed a year's curriculum in six months, which says a lot more for the pupil/teacher ratio and Orla's forbearance than for our teaching skills.

As the year went on, we vowed that we would never again attempt to teach our own children and that Orla should go to the *demotikon* in Parikia the following September. After all, one of the most important aspects of schooling for young children is socialisation. Orla needed the companionship of children of her own age and certainly she needed more patient and objective teachers than her parents. Besides, if we were to stay in Greece for a considerable period, we thought that we had better integrate both ourselves and the children into Parian society.

To do that we had to learn Greek.

During our first winter on the island a group of local intellectuals founded a cultural society named after Archilocus, the satirical poet who is said to have invented iambic poetry. He was born in Paros in the middle of the seventh century BC. (Paros, then, was a good place for Rory who was writing poetry, some of it quite satirical.) The society, which we joined, met every month to listen to lectures on Greek literature, given by one of the Parian intellectuals or by a visiting scholar, or to watch some esoteric film which would be followed by a discussion session. A sizeable proportion of the audience at these meetings consisted of foreign residents, a few of whom spoke excellent Greek and who could therefore understand the proceedings and participate in the discussions. The majority, like ourselves, struggled with this, one of the most difficult of European languages, in my view at any rate.

Of course, we knew the many Greek-origin words in

English, in the terminology of medicine, psychology and philosophy. Nonetheless, as I was discovering, ordinary conversational Greek is neither as easy to speak nor to understand as Spanish, French or Italian are. Maybe it is because the different script is daunting. Certainly, the grammar is very difficult. Whatever the reason, many of the foreign residents we knew over the years did not get past the most rudimentary of Greek conversational phrases such as *Kali mera* or *Yiassou* and the vocabulary for basic food and drink. Even fewer could read or write the language beyond the most basic shop signs and place names.

Because I could only speak and understand the simplest Greek words and phrases, it was rather difficult for me to make any meaningful contact with Parians. There were, at that time, only a few Greeks on the island who could speak English. French was still the only foreign language taught at secondary school. Perhaps the language problem was one of the reasons why the foreign residents tended to congregate together and to mix with those few Greeks who spoke English and who wanted to spend some of their time with the *xenia*.

My progress in the language was painfully slow and tortuous, especially during the first few months. I would get out my books dutifully every day and attempt to learn new verbs and vocabulary. Then I would practise these on our long-suffering neighbours, Elias, Maria and Eleni, and on the shopkeepers in the village. That got me so far but then, when I could make myself understood regarding daily greetings and our shopping needs, I seemed to reach a low plateau from which it was extremely difficult to climb further. As I like learning languages, I felt very frustrated by my lack of progress in Greek. The fact that the only radio

78

station we listened to was the World Service of the BBC did not help, nor did the fact that I read only English books. The result was that the only occasions on which I was forced to speak Greek was with our neighbours, with our landlord, and with the shopkeepers in Parikia.

Still, I tried my best to push myself up from my low linguistic base camp. I spent hours every evening struggling with the alphabet and trying to find some hook on which I could hang the new words and phrases I was learning, so that I would remember them. My progress was not assisted by the innate politeness of our Greek neighbours which prevented them from ever correcting me, so that I went on making the same mistakes in grammar and pronunciation for ages. They seemed to be so pleased that a foreigner was making an effort to learn their language that they kept congratulating me on how well I spoke Greek!

Self-study with books was not doing the job. I needed a Greek teacher but, even if there had been one on Paros, I could not have afforded to pay for lessons. I decided to use the barter system. I offered to teach English to Stamatis, a young potter who had recently returned from his studies in Italy and was planning to set up a studio on his native Paros. In return he would give me Greek lessons. That worked reasonably well for a few months until the pottery business took off and Stamatis became too busy in his studio. I think that he might have got the better end of the bargain: I was a qualified teacher and that does make a difference. Stamatis found it difficult to explain the building-blocks of his language clearly to me and he did not quite know how to structure lessons sequentially, so that I ended up trying to teach him how to teach me Greek as well as giving him English lessons. Years later, due to the sheer necessity of his having to speak English to the thousands of annual visitors to his very popular ceramics studio and shop, Stamatis's English is almost fluent while my Greek remains a rather creaky communications vehicle.

It was not, in fact, until Orla went to the *demotikon*, the village primary school, in our second year on Paros, that I was forced to shift off that plateau in order to be able to communicate with her teacher and with the other parents. and to be able to help her with her homework.

Native English speakers are frequently accused of being too lazy or too arrogant to learn other languages. While this may be true of some language imperialists, I think the charge is both unfair and untrue with regard to most native English speakers. There are a several major deterrents to our ability to speak other languages. One of the main obstacles is the fact that nearly everywhere in the world people want to learn English and therefore seem to regard native English speakers as free language teachers and objects of practice. Secondly, no matter what part of the world you find yourself in, it is hard to escape the domination of the English language: films, pop songs, advertisements and other forms of popular culture are very often in English. In Greece, for instance, few Hollywood films shown in the cinemas or on television are dubbed so that, unless you can read the Greek subtitles quickly, you follow the films in English and learn no Greek.

I have had many experiences in Greece over the years in which I would address a shopkeeper or waiter in Greek, the grammar and syntax of which would be correct – even if my accent and Northern European looks clearly identified me as a foreigner – only to have them reply in broken English.

One day, exasperated by such an incident, I said to a shopkeeper in Greek, "Excuse me, could you tell me which language I spoke to you in and which language I am speaking now?"

Startled, he looked at me and said, in Greek, "Eh . . . Greek . . . I suppose."

"And do you understand clearly what I'm saying in Greek?"

"Yes, I do, it's clear Greek, very good."

"Then why, may I ask, did you reply to me in English?"

"I don't know. Maybe it is because you don't look Greek and I just don't expect foreigners to speak our language."

I did not learn classical Greek at school, so, no doubt, I would have had similar difficulties in communicating with Archilochus or other BC residents of Paros. Although I suspect that in those days Greeks expected foreigners to speak their language.

Paros is an ancient land. The spirits of other islanders from past centuries are all around. Worshippers in white pleated tunics stand behind the shadow of the sun on the sites of ancient temples. The short, rough lives of the slaves who quarried heavy tons of translucent marble for the Parthenon have left their traces in the rock seams. The shouts of sailors and pirates who sailed into Parian harbours echo in the winding streets.

I wanted to know something about the people whose spirits lingered near me on high places where lofty Doric-columned temples once looked out on the same sea. And I wanted to know, too, what other travellers thought about the island. Ernle Bradford, whom Lawrence Durrell once described as "an enviable mixture of sea-dog, poet and scholar" visited Paros first in the 1940s and wrote the following:

"Inland from Paros (Parikia) the country everywhere has a calm and sculptural feel that is distinctive of Paros. This is an island which would cure the jangled nerves of city-dwellers, for it is peaceful, without being enervating . . . The Parians, in fact, are a cheerful breed of islanders, less commercialised than the Mykonos people and not so dour as the men of Siphnos."

When we arrived on Paros in 1977, it was still true that Paros was much less commercialised than Mykonos and that the island would soothe the jangled nerves of stressed-out urbanites. Whether Parians were more cheerful than the natives of Siphnos was a point of discussion with our Parian neighbours, who agreed with Bradford. It may be true of all small places, whether islands or inland villages – the people of the next island or village are considered to be meaner, less cheerful or less hard-working than the natives of the one you live in. Certainly, later on during our stay on the island, when we would tell our neighbours on Paros that we were going to visit the next-door island of Naxos, less than half an hour's boat journey away, they would say, "But what do you want to go there for? Those Naxiots are not friendly, not friendly at all. And they'll do their best to cheat you, so watch out."

However, when we visited Naxos we found charming, independent-minded people who did not seem either to need or to want the level or kind of tourism which, though in its infancy, was growing rapidly on Paros at the end of the seventies.

Sir Charles Napier, a contemporary and friend of Byron and an equally fervent Hellenophile, made no distinctions among the Greeks, finding them all equally charming. In a remark which somehow endears him to me, despite the politically incorrect reference to my people, he wrote:

> "The merry Greeks are worth all the other nations put together. I like to see them, to hear them; I like their fun, their good humour, their paddy ways – for they are very like Irishmen. All their bad habits are Venetian, but their wit, their eloquence and their good nature are all their own."

I have been compared to a Greek only a few times in all our years on Paros. On one of these occasions there was a petrol shortage, an annual event in the summer which seems to bring out the xenophobia in petrol-station owners. I was patiently queuing with my empty moped at the only petrol station which still had petrol supplies in the searing noonday heat, when only mad dogs and people desperate for petrol were out. The large expensive Land Rover in front of me had its capacious tank filled to overflowing and then the Greek driver handed a giant jerrycan to the plump young pump attendant. The sun blazed down. I waited, the sun beat a tom-tom drum in my brain. My turn came. I had my tiny tank filled and then gave the attendant the three-litre plastic container I had brought to get petrol for Rory's empty motor-bike.

"Only tanks," he snapped, going over to the next customer who was driving a truck.

"Excuse me," I replied calmly, sweat trickling saltily down my face, "I have a very small tank in my motor-bike, it takes very little petrol. What do you mean 'only tanks'? I've just seen you fill a great big jerrycan for that guy in the Land-Rover. So, now please fill this small container for me."

It was as if I had not spoken, as if I had become

invisible. The attendant, the surly-looking teenage son of the owner, went on filling other motorists' tanks and jerrycans. The sun was an open furnace. My sandals stuck to the melting tarmac. I braced myself against the hot metal of my moped. I exploded. In my most fluent Greek, I lambasted the surly one. Who did he think he was? What did he think he was doing? Was there one rule which applied to Greeks and another to foreigners? Well, I had been coming to this island since before he was born and I demanded my share of petrol, just like everyone else. If I did not get it at once, I would set the police on him. I'd . . . I'd . . . I spluttered into incoherence.

Silence descended on the petrol station. The Greeks in the unruly queue sat back to enjoy the spectacle, while the foreigners looked on in incomprehension at another "typical" Greek encounter. Surly son looked around for support, suspended between his natural belligerence and bewilderment at my outburst. The owner and his wife came running out of the garage. The father grabbed the pump from his glowering son. The mother made smoothing movements in the air with her hands as if she were about to calm a difficult child.

"Don't worry, you'll get your petrol," she cooed. "We know who you are now. You live here. Isterni, isn't it? Near the Roussos. You Irish are so like us Greeks. So explosive, so quick-tempered."

I left the station before I gave them the benefit of my thoughts on the similarities between the Greeks and the Irish. I must have some bad Venetian habits, too.

One of the attractions of Paros for me was the fact that it had such a long history, that people like Archilocus had lived and written his satirical poetry on the island. I learned from Bradford that Paros had been home to other

84

quite well-known residents in classical times. Evenos, for instance, who lived at the end of the fifth century BC, was a philosopher and a teacher of Socrates, as well as a poet. A whole brace of sculptors lived here also, Thrasymedes and Skopas being two of the best known.

It is no wonder that Paros attracted sculptors, for Paros is a marble island. I went to Marathi, a few kilometres into the hills outside Parikia, with Annie on one of my OFF days to see the ancient marble mines. They had been closed for years, but we were able to go down into one of the main shafts. The sense of the presence of others was powerful. The laboured breathing of the hundreds of slaves who, from the sixth century BC, had quarried the great slabs of marble from this rock face and somehow got it up that steep slope to be transported to all parts of the Greek world, was a whispering echo in the cavernous darkness. And the dozens of disturbed bats that flew over our heads made swooshing noises with their wings which spoke of perennial shivers in this dark place. And I thought of how such beautiful, white, translucent marble is taken from such a dank, dark place, like beautiful spring flowers from the hard cold ground of winter.

On my next free day I followed the marble trail to the small archaeological museum in Parikia to see the most famous marble artefact remaining on Paros. The Parian Chronicle (581-264 BC) is an outline of Greek cultural history carved on marble slabs and consisting of ninety-three lines written in the Attic dialect. The Chronicle records important events such as the births and deaths of poets, including that of Homer, dates of festivals and when different kinds of poetry were introduced. Like so many Greek treasures, only a fragment of the Parian Chronicle is still to be seen its native place. The rest of it is now in the Ashmolean in Oxford. As I read the inscriptions in the museum and learned of the whereabouts of most of the Chronicle, I thought again of the arguments of ex-singer and Greek government minister, Melina Melcouri, among others who have argued so passionately for the return of Greek treasures to where they came from. She was, of course, particularly known for her battle with the British authorities for the return to Greece of what the British call the Elgin and what the Greeks call the Parthenon marbles. It makes sense that antiquities should be located in the places for which they were made. On the other hand, if museums started returning everything to where it originated, where would it all end? I gave up the argument with myself and went off to Dinosaki's for a coffee.

As I walked through the village streets with marble on my mind, I noticed how little remained of the marble heritage of Paros. Little that was obvious, at any rate, except in the district called the Kastro, which is an acropolis overlooking the sea, not far from the port. Here the great drums and slices of fluted columns from the temple of Hera form the walls of a Venetian castle. And the villagers have incorporated bits and pieces of ancient marble from the temple into their houses. Here there is a section of a marble column forming the pedestal for that concrete table top. Over there the lintel of that house is an ancient slab of marble. In fact there are so many marble remains lying about in old walls, or under the foundations of houses, that it is not possible to excavate anywhere in order to build without finding some piece of antique marble. If the find is reported to the police or to the museum, then all building work is halted until the find is properly excavated. So people are tempted to say nothing and simply incorporate the find into the new walls of their building.

Outside Parikia there are few remains from antiquity. Little intact or standing upright. A few tumbled stones, remnants of shrines to Apollo and Aphrodite, lie scattered among the poppies. But no doubt the ground is full of hidden treasures. Recently, for instance, a number of marble sarcophagi were uncovered during road construction and a whole cemetery was subsequently unearthed beside the port.

Sitting sipping my coffee in Dinosaki's, in a state of nostalgic reverie, I thought about former inhabitants of this island. In classical times I knew that the population had been much higher than it was in 1978. Twenty thousand as compared with seven thousand. I supposed that so many more people were needed in those days, to work the marble quarries, to man the shipping fleets, to trade, to control the seas around the Cyclades and to protect the island from invasions. For these little islands were sovereign states with their own administration and defense forces. The Parians had a reputation for being opportunists, for changing sides during the many wars, against the Persians and others. But they had to survive and there is no crime in that.

Still, there was a period when they did not survive on Paros, when the island was practically deserted during periods in the eighteenth century. There was another great exodus after the Second World War. As in so many islands and villages all over Greece and in rural areas throughout Europe, the decline in subsistence agriculture, rising unemployment and the magnet of bright city lights emptied the countryside of young active people who went off to the cities or abroad to find work, leaving their grandparents to wander the childless streets in crumbling villages.

I finished my cold coffee, switched off my mental musings on history and decided it was time to get to know more about modern Paros and the Parians of my own day.

Chapter Seven

Spring

The long winter days, when it grew dark and cold at three o'clock in the afternoon, slowly brightened until it seemed that the world was made of light and flowers. The whole island became an oriental carpet. Flowers bloomed in every field, along the roadsides, in every crack and corner: brilliant white and yellow daisies, hypnotic red poppies, a child's paintbox of sweet-smelling anemones.

I had been happy on sunny winter days phoning dreary Belfast from a phone box beside the sparkling sea, but being in Greece in spring for the first time was pure magic. The newness of the light, the colours and scents of the wild flowers, the sheer profusion of it all delighted me beyond measure. I filled every jamjar with flowers and put them all over the house, pressed petals between the leaves of books, and painted pictures of flowers in my journal. I taught the children the names of those flowers I knew, and looked up those I had never seen before in a book on the flora and fauna of Greece. I could hardly contain my pleasure. Spring was never so happy. I wanted to lie in those blossoming fields forever, with the flowers blooming eternally, no petals drooping, no leaves wilting, no sun going down, no getting old, forever in the land of *Tír na nÓg*.

In our garden, the orange, lemon, and almond-trees were bent over with blossoms like curtsying ladies in pink and white crinolines. Different parts of the island produced their own floral speciality. In some areas purply-blue Cretan irises waved in triumph. In other places, the delicious perfume of narcissi and rock roses scented the warming air. And nearly everywhere, wild garlic, purple vetch, white-bearded asphodels and grape hyacinths created an Impressionists' paradise. It was like living in a Monet painting. Everything – houses, mountains, valleys, the sea, the whole landscape – had a primeval clarity, a rinsed freshness, a sense of being renewed. Persephone returned from the Underworld.

Just to open the back door of Villa Ariadne in the mornings and to look out over the flowering trees, out over the poppied fields starred with daisies, and down to the glinting sea gladdened your heart and filled your lungs with a sigh of pleasure.

Gradually we began to remove the layers of clothes that had kept us from freezing all winter. On days when the sun was unexpectedly warm we were down to jeans and T-shirts. Orla and Fiona hunted out their swimsuits, but it was still a little too early for swimming.

Time to whitewash the house for Easter. To whitewash also between the paving stones on the terrace at the front of the house. Time to clean the winter grime from the windows. Time to throw open the house again to the smell of the fields and the sea.

Time also to open up ourselves and to begin to participate more in the life of the community among whom we had come to live. All winter we had more or less hibernated with the foreign community and our immediate Greek neighbours, Elias and his family. We had not begun to take part in what was going on in the Greek community. Now that our knowledge of Greek had improved somewhat, it was time, we agreed, to get to know more native Parians and more about their way of life.

The first opportunity we found to participate in the life of the local community was at *Apokreas*, the Greek Carnival, when children dress in fancy costumes and adults dance in the tavernas. We decided that we would dress our children in fancy costumes, too, so that they could take part in the festivities. It was quite a challenge to make fancy dress for the girls from the few clothes and materials we possessed. The field outside our bedroom window gave me the inspiration I needed. What better than to use the flowering gifts of nature in spring time to transform Orla and Fiona into diminutive Primaveras. They unearthed their flowery summer dresses from the bottom of the wardrobe and we all went into the field and gathered armfuls of wild flowers. Then we laced wreaths of anemones and hyacinths through their blonde hair and wrapped bracelets of daisies around their wrists. They were spring from head to toe and very excited.

The square in Parikia was full of little Greek children, all in elaborate fancy dress. There were dozens of princesses with medieval coifs and trailing veils, of Robin Hoods in doublets and forest-green hats, of fairy queens with wings and wands, of well-armed cowboys and Indians. All wearing ready-made, shop-bought costumes. When our two Primaveras joined the throng, one of the Robin Hoods started laughing and pointed them out to his friends and parents. Then the princesses laughed and pointed and soon the copycat cowboys and Indians joined in the ridicule. Fiona did not understand what was going on and laughed with her mockers. But her big sister was bitterly disappointed and hurt.

"What's wrong with me and Fifi?" she asked us. "Why are they all laughing and pointing at us? Is it because our costumes are different?"

When something cruel happens to my children, I feel much more angry than if it had happened to myself. Seeing the hurt in the eyes of a small child must release primitive protective instincts. I wanted to shout at those Greek children. I wanted to say that anyone can go into a shop and buy a silly princess outfit, all you need is money and a complete lack of imagination. I wanted to tell them that creativity is about making something of your own and not copying everyone else. But, of course, I said nothing. I could not have said all that in grammatical Greek in any case, and I certainly was not going to draw any further adverse attention to my family.

Rory and I gathered in our blossoming children, assured them that they looked lovely, much prettier than any commercial princess, and took them off to Dinosaki's, where we treated them to the largest bowls of ice cream and a sticky *baklava* pastry each. Rory and I drank a cognac to calm us down. What disappointed me most about the whole episode was that not one of the older children or the parents intervened in the childish mockery of two little foreigners. As an outsider, it is not easy to participate in any small community. You do not know the more subtle rules and your well-meaning attempts to integrate can backfire or be misunderstood. We adults may be able to take rejection or censure with varying degrees of sang froid, but children are vulnerable and easily hurt by thoughtless exclusion.

The next opportunity to participate in a Greek event was soon after *Apokreas*. Penelope invited me to accompany her to a wedding. Nothing could go wrong, I thought. I would find out what was expected of wedding guests and learn a few phrases to congratulate the couple and their parents and another few new phrases to get me through the small talk at the wedding feast.

It was a sort of a shotgun wedding. During the carnival period a young man from the hillside village of Kostos fell in love with a fourteen-year-old peasant girl from Kolimbithres, a beautiful bay near Naoussa. The young couple were determined to marry. But when Romeo went to Juliet's parents to ask for her hand, he was not only forbidden to marry her, he was ordered never to see her again. His family was not well-off and he had no land. A few nights later, on a dark night when the moon was a just a mere sliver of silver, the young man from Kostos kidnapped his willing Kolimbithres girl. Clinging to his red motor-bike, they sped away from her sleeping farmhouse, dust and gravel spewing from the wheels. If the couple could remain undetected for three days, her parents would be forced to agree to the marriage. The girl's honour would be deemed to have been tainted and her family would require an immediate wedding to save face.

The pair managed to escape the hunt by the girl's father, brothers and uncles. Food and water was brought to their secret hideout by trusted friends and, when they emerged from hiding after four days, the date of the wedding was fixed in a hurry.

When Penelope, who was a friend of the bride's family,

suggested that I might like to go to the wedding with her, I hesitated and said, "I'd really love to go, but I haven't anything formal enough to wear at a wedding."

"Weddings here aren't all that formal," Penelope replied. "This wedding, especially, won't be very formal, the families aren't rich, so wear anything except jeans and boots."

So I concocted a wedding outfit from my hippy Indian-cotton skirt and an embroidered blouse and waistcoat, which I borrowed from Phoebe Wheeler. Gloria insisted that I borrow her gold, high-heeled strappy shoes. On the afternoon of the wedding, Penelope and I met at the bus station in Parikia to catch a bus to Kostos where the ceremony was to take place.

It was an unseasonably cold day and I shivered in my flimsy clothes while we waited for the bus. I probably looked like someone in fancy dress, but I did not care. It felt great to get out of those jeans, those shapeless sweaters and those big boots. The bus was late. The wind blew up. I was forced to don my anorak which rather spoiled the effect.

Kostos is a small village of about three hundred people in the hills about eight kilometres above Parikia, looking out towards Naxos. It was formerly a Venetian lookout for pirates and enemy ships. The village church of Ayios Pantelemon, its beautifully carved *iconostasis* glowing in the candlelight, was filled to the doors with the families of the bride and groom, none of whom looked at all put out by the enforced nature of the wedding which was about to be celebrated.

I need not have worried about my wedding costume. This was no fashion parade. The mothers of the bride and groom wore nondescript, shapeless, black dresses; the

94

uniform, it seems, of so many Greek women over fifty. In many parts of Greece, people, especially the women, wear black mourning clothes for years after the deaths of their parents or siblings. Between the ages of forty and fifty many people lose their parents and this is the reason why women of that age wear a black uniform. The mothers were obviously mourning some family member and even the occasion of their children's wedding had not got them out of their black weeds. Their grey-streaked hair was scraped into fat buns at the nape of their necks and they carried large white handkerchiefs, which came in handy for expected tears. The two moustached fathers were also dressed in black and looked most uncomfortable in unfamiliar, stiffly-starched white shirts and strangling neckties. The young male guests wore the ubiquitous jeans and white shirts of young men from Kansas to Kostos while the girls were festive in frilly summer dresses which they had been obliged to cover up with woollen cardigans against the chilly March day.

As one who had been brought up in the rather strict formality of Catholic church services, I found the Orthodox wedding ceremony in Kostos quite noisy and informal. While the two priests intoned and chanted the liturgy, shook incense holders and kissed icons, people drifted in and out of the small church, buying candles as they entered, lighting them in front of icons, kissing the icons, and chatting in loud whispers to their neighbours. The bride and groom, oblivious of the singing priests, exchanged meaningful whispers and looks throughout the ceremony while the bride's mother, like a fussy hen, ran back and forth, picking imaginary threads from her daughter's dress and constantly adjusting her long veil. The two fathers were engrossed in conversation which involved much gesticulation with spatula-shaped, work-worn hands. Young men chatted up young women at the back of the church. Arranging new trysts perhaps. The atmosphere was one of easy conviviality. Neighbours gossiped and the religious business, it seemed to me, was conducted as a theatrical backdrop to the other proceedings.

Everyone fell silent however, when the *stephanes*, the wedding wreaths, were held aloft over the heads of the bride and groom in turn and then exchanged, backwards and forwards, several times. Then the priests, the young couple, the bridesmaid and the best man, all linked together with white ribbons, began an animated circular dance around the altar, while the congregation showered the couple with rice and shouted congratulations, *Na zieste, Na zieste*! (May you live!) The groom, a tall, brown-skinned young man of about twenty-five, with glistening black hair and triumphant tawny eyes, lifted his head and surveyed the congregation, especially his new in-laws, like a victorious lion. The bride, a shy, slim teenager, with doe's eyes and long ebony hair which fell in waves to her waist, seemed overwhelmed by all the attention she was receiving.

On leaving the church, each guest was presented with the traditional wedding bundle of sugared almonds tied up in white veiling with a satin ribbon. I did not know the significance of the almonds. Rice for fertility, nuts for what? Sweetness perhaps? Or maybe fertility too, the nut being the kernel of life. Perhaps they were the equivalent of the pieces of wedding cake you put under your pillow to dream of your ideal lover.

By taxi, bus, car, donkey and motor-bike the wedding guests then made their way to the wedding reception at the bride's home, a journey of about ten kilometres, around the

Picking flowers for the Primaveras, Spring 1978.

Weaving in the garden of Villa Ariadne with Fiona and Orla, March 1979.

The "Grannies" with Orla and Fiona, Villa Ariadne, 1978.

Villa Ariadne.

As it was . . . is . . . but will not remain! Isterni, March 1979.

Manolis and Evangelis bringing up the supplies
by donkey to re-build Isterni.

Rory with Pandelis, Isterni.

Our dear friends, Zacharias and Maria, Roussos.

Vasilis the potter, Sifnos, 1978.

Vasilis the potter, twenty years on with Fionnuala, Sifnos.

View from the house in Isterni, 1992.

Fiona, Orla, Fionnuala and Rory, Parikia, 1988.

Rory at breakfast in Isterni, 1992.

bay of Naoussa, to the farm beside the old abandoned monastery of Ayios Johannis. The wedding feast was prepared in the courtyard. Kids and lambs roasted on spits over great fires along with several chickens. Home-made wine was ladled out from wooden barrels. Salads, plates of bean stew and hunks of bread were laid on trestle tables in the big farmhouse kitchen. There was enough food to feed the army of Alexander the Great. It is a matter of pride and honour for Greeks to provide groaning tables of food and drink for their guests.

So the wedding feast continued into the night under the Milky Way and the whole heaven full of stars. Waves rolled in loud congratulation around the bay below the farm. Dogs and cats fought for scraps of bone and gristle thrown by guests in the dim courtyard. Donkeys and mules brayed mournfully from the posts to which they were tethered. This was a Rembrandt painting, all velvet browns, lit by globs of golden lamplight, the shadowy figures of wedding guests forming the backdrop to the action in the foreground, the bride and groom and their families eating their wedding feast at a table in the centre of the kitchen.

When the meal was over, the tables were dismantled and the floor was cleared for dancing. A piper played shrill music on a bagpipe made from a sheep's belly. Maruso, the bride's mother, sang a traditional wedding song with about twenty verses and everyone, except me, took up the chorus. Giorgos, the father of the bride, sang another, shorter song, more risque than his wife's, judging by the chortles of the men around me. Then the young couple led us into the dance. First of all they danced with each other, next with both sets of parents, then with guests in turn, as in a Paul Jones. The dance music was provided by an unusual trio, by the piper on his home-made bagpipes, by another musician blowing what looked like a cow's horn, and by a third on a saucepan-shaped drum. Their music was as insistent, rhythmic, swirling and hypnotic as Arab music. They played *ballos*. We had to dance.

Ballos, the island dances, are much easier for an inept foreigner to learn than the flamboyant Zorba-style *sirtaki*. Penelope and I danced on and on, fuelled by the strong red wine and only stopping for long enough to catch our breath and to go outside occasionally for a gulp of cold night air.

The only foreigners at the wedding were Penelope, myself and an American painter, a long-time island resident who knew the parents of the groom. I did not know him well, I had met him a few times with Penelope in Parikia. I gathered he was *persona non grata* at many parties and in many houses. He was a tall, thin, wiry fellow with squinting marmalade eyes who looked as if he never had a decent meal and ate cigarettes for breakfast. There was something unsavoury about him. He reminded me of an animal, a rattlesnake maybe, or a coyote.

I never saw his paintings; he said he could not be bothered exhibiting them on Paros where people were not able to appreciate them. Penelope told me that in all the time she had known him she had never seen any of his work. Whatever he did, he did it in his studio, which was supposed to be in the stables of the house he rented near Naoussa. Every time I saw him he was drunk and I wondered if he was ever sober enough to paint. He was something of a nomad, with no permanent address in the United States. He left the island from time to time and nobody knew where he went, on what business, or if or when he might return. Voluble, gregarious, flamboyantly entertaining, he was addicted to contentiousness. On the night of the wedding, after a day's heavy drinking, he stumbled around the floor trying to dance, pausing every so often to flick the tassel of his *berata* out of his eyes. With his swashbuckling manner, his black moustache and his vermillion *berata* he looked like a nineteenth-century Greek freedom fighter during the War of Independence.

"You are to be my second, Fionnuala," he called across the dancers to me.

"Your what?"

"My second, woman. I'm about to fight a duel. I need a second."

"Oh for God's sake, sober up and don't be making a disgrace of yourself. This is a wedding feast, not a pub brawl," I snapped at him.

I had no interest whatsoever in finding out the cause of the row, so I moved off to the far end of the room. He staggered after me, shouting, "The butcher, Petros, has insulted me. Insulted my country. My honour demands a duel."

Then, picking up a carving-knife from a table, he weaved his way through the dancing couples towards the butcher, brandishing the knife above his head like one of Ali Baba's thieves.

Petros, our landlord's agent, was a powerfully built man, as strong as a Spanish bull. He could make mincemeat of the emaciated drunken American who was twice his age.

"What's all this about, Petros?" I felt obliged to intervene in order to prevent an international incident.

"This crazy *malakas* came in front of me. He spilled wine on the floor. 'This is your blood I spill,' he shouted. I can't accept this insult, so we must fight outside."

"Don't mind him, he's drunk, you can see that. He

didn't mean what he said, he doesn't even know what he's saying or what he's doing," I apologised on behalf of my fellow-foreigner.

While I was trying to appease the enraged butcher in the kitchen, the purple-faced painter was prancing around outside the door, whirling the flashing kitchen-knife above his head and calling in to Petros, "Butcher, come out here. Choose your seconds, *malakas*. The duel will take place. Fight like a man."

The music droned to a sudden halt. The horrified wedding guests stopped dancing and stood around in consternation. Greeks hate brawls and despise those who cannot handle alcohol. Suddenly the bride's brothers lunged forward and grabbed the whirling dervish painter and bundled him out of the courtyard. The bride's parents asked Penelope and me to get rid of him, to take him away from their home. And so we had to leave the wedding and drag the plastered painter along the dark track back to his house in the village. I was angry because, although Penelope and I had done nothing wrong, I felt that we were leaving the wedding feast branded with the disgrace of a drunken, abusive foreigner. Of course, I did not know what the butcher had said or done. I could not find out, either, as the would-be duellist had no recollection whatsoever of the incident when next I met him in Naoussa.

Penelope told me afterwards that the bride's family were deeply upset and very angry. They felt the wedding had been dishonoured by the drunken brawl, and especially by the threatened use of knives. It would bring bad luck to the young married couple, they believed. With foreigners like that on the island, no wonder integration into the Greek community was not too easy.

Nonetheless, we were determined not to be put off and to participate in the Greek life of the island as much as we could. For what is the point of living somewhere if you stay in a familiar cocoon, only mixing with other foreigners, speaking only your own language, dancing your own dances and listening to your own music?

Springtime in Greece is full of feasts and celebration. March 25th is *Evangelismos tis Theotiokoi*, the Annunciation of the Angel to the Virgin Mary. It is also Greek Independence Day and marks the beginning of the final revolt against the Ottoman Empire in 1821. Throughout Greece, schoolchildren parade through the streets in national costume and folk dances are performed in the open air. We went into Parikia to see how Independence Day would be celebrated there.

Along the waterfront hundreds of people walked in a colourful procession, waving the blue and white flag of Greece and wearing costumes their great grandparents might have worn in the nineteenth century. The women wore long full skirts of rich fabrics like brocade, white, full-sleeved, embroidered blouses, and heavily decorated felt or velvet waistcoats. The men were resplendent in white tights, white shirts, embroidered waistcoats and multicoloured *zionari*, or sashes. On their heads they wore the *berata*. Anyone who has seen the changing of the guard outside the old palace in Syntagma Square in Athens will recognise the male costume.

When the procession and speeches were over, a band played dance music on a platform in front of the Town Hall. The Greeks know how to celebrate and they love festivals. They especially love dancing and everyone believes they can dance. Perhaps not the preening male-only *sirtaki*, but certainly the many folk dances of the

101

islands. I have yet to see a Greek, male or female, no matter how old, plump or ungainly-looking, who can not dance with elegance and grace.

In Ireland, which is famous for music and dance, our traditional dancing seems to me to be more studied, more controlled, even wooden. Despite the fact that many of us went to Irish dancing classes as children, and some of us took part in *feiseanna* in our elaborate Celtic embroidered costumes with our hair tortured into fat ringlets, how few of us have the grace and confidence to dance as adults! In recent years, however, with the marvellous revival in interest in set dancing throughout the country and among all age groups, the stiffness is beginning to go out of our dancing as more and more of us join in the sets. I would like to think that the self-conscious awkwardness of body we have inherited might not pass on to the next generation and we might all dance like Greeks.

Young and old danced to celebrate Greek Independence and we, too, were dragged into a laughing group and taught the basic steps by Paniotis, the grocer from whom we bought the best olives. Penelope and Jean-Pierre were dancing expertly in the next group and I could see Deborah busily sketching the scene from her usual table outside Dinosaki's.

Elias and his family invited us to join them in a picnic in the countryside near Pounda, where they had relatives, to celebrate *Katheri Deftera* (Clean Monday), the beginning of Lent. We were to eat Lenten food, they said, which meant there would be no meat or olive-oil. I was interested to know how many people on Paros still observed the Lenten fast. Elias told me that only the older citizens like himself and Maria still observed the no meat, no cheese, no oil rule.

Katheri Deftera was a sunny day and the sea shone like a newly-washed blue plate beyond the meadow where we gathered for the picnic: Elias and Maria, Eleni, her married sister Aspacia, Elias's sister and her young family, Rory, myself and our children. Having to speak Greek all afternoon was difficult for myself and Rory, but Orla and Fiona seemed to have no trouble at all in understanding the rules of the games they were playing with the Greek children.

Maria spread out a feast of shellfish, *laganes* (flat bread), garlic and *horta*, which was like dandelion leaves sprinkled with lemon juice. Everything we ate was produced on the farm by our hosts and Elias had got the shellfish from the rocks around the beach at Delfini. I really enjoyed the simple food, it tasted fresh and light, exactly right for spring.

On *Megalo Pempti* (Holy Thursday), Orla and Fiona were very excited because they were allowed to go to the Ekatonpyliani to see the start of the Easter ceremonies. Maybe they thought that chocolate Easter eggs would be distributed. However, after half an hour or so of listening to the solemn reading from the passion of Christ, they became restless and wandered around the church and out into the courtyard. We did not have to worry about their safety; dozens of old *yaias*, grandmothers, were only too pleased to fuss over them and make sure they did not wander too far away.

Our children were happy enough to be brought back to the lovely old church the following day, *Megali Paraskevi*, (Good Friday), where we saw the figure of Christ being removed from the cross and put into the *epitaphos* or coffin, which was magnificently decorated with hundreds of spring flowers. The choir sang laments and suddenly we were covered in thousands of rose petals which came drifting down in a sweet and scented shower from the dome of the basilica. Birth in death, sweetness in sorrow, hope in despair, all the paradoxes of life, richly symbolised.

I stood in the centuries-old Byzantine church with the smell of incense pickling my nostrils and the sound of chanting reverberating in my brain. I could not help wondering whether, in this secular age in which our children were being raised, there was something which adequately replaces such rich ritual and symbolism. How important is public ritual to mark life's passages: birth, marriage, death? Is the ordinary prose of life sufficient to sustain the soul? Are not some richly embellished capital letters and scrolls, some celebrations, some rituals, some symbols, needed to save the manuscript from being a flat, dull, consumerist pamphlet?

When Christ was in his coffin, the black-bearded priests in their rich vestments carried it through the church and out into the courtyard. The entire congregation followed the procession of the coffin through the village streets from the Ekatonpyliani to the modern church of Zoodochos Pigi at the far end of Parikia.

We wanted to see the celebrations through to the end, so on the night of *Megalo Savato* (Easter Saturday) we wrapped the children up warmly and brought them once again to the ceremonies in the Ekatonpyliani. Like the Greek children around them, Orla and Fiona fell fast asleep in our arms, lullabied by the singing priests and warmed by the hundreds of candles the congregation held to greet the risen Christ. Just before midnight all the candles were blown out. For a moment we stood silently in warm darkness as before the sepulchre. Then the bishop, having relit his candle from the Pascal flame, sang out,

Kristos anesti! (Christ is risen!) to which the whole congregation replied *Alithos anesti!* (Indeed He is risen!) The Pascal flame was then passed from candle to candle until the whole church once again blazed with light.

The resurrection of Christ was announced in the courtyard of the basilica in an explosion of fireworks which lit the void of the night sky with festive, fiery flashes. We left the church, shaking hands with anyone we knew and agreeing that indeed Christ had risen. Captain Peter was waiting for us and invited us to his house for a very welcome warming bowl of *magheritsa*, Easter soup made from the tripe of lambs. We did not tell the children what the ingredients of the soup were and they drank it greedily.

The *Paska* festivities were not yet over. On Easter Sunday we slept in after our late night at the church and in Captain Peter's. In the afternoon we set out to walk four or five miles to the house of two German friends who had invited us, along with the whole foreign community, to celebrate Easter in traditional Greek style. We carried bottles of Elias's wine, chunks of Maria's *kaseri* cheese and sleeping bags for the overnight stay. Up past the wooded site of the monastery of Christos sto Dhassos (Christ in the Woods) we climbed, along a tortuous donkey-path to the beautiful two-hundred-year old farmhouse where Klaus and Bettina lived. It was a very simple house, without electricity or running water. The floors were beaten earth, the cupboards were deep niches in the thick stone walls. Delicious sweet-tasting spring water was drawn up in a bucket from a deep well in the middle of the kitchen floor. Outside on the terrace a kid was being roasted on a spit and the other guests were showing off the patterns on the red-dyed eggs they had decorated for Easter.

105

When the meat was roasted we spread out the food and wine which we had brought on tables under an enormous plane tree. We filled our glasses with *mavro krasi* or *retsina*, we piled a mountain of food on our plates and lay feasting in happy groups on a Persian carpet of brilliant yellow daisies, blood-red poppies and tiny purple and pink orchids. And we told ourselves that this indeed was the Lotus Land and we were the Lotus-eaters.

Chapter Eight

English Lessons

Lotus-eaters are not supposed to suffer from toothaches. However, after a week of nagging pain, I was forced to find a dentist in the village. That was how I really got to know more of the Greeks on Paros.

Eleni was one of two dentists in Parikia and a friend of Andreas, our scandalised neighbour, so I went to her. She was a very pretty woman in her mid-twenties, not long finished her dentistry studies. I do not know why I was so surprised that the surgery she worked in was as modern as that of my own dentist in Dublin. Eleni was gentle and efficient and I was so well pleased with the speedy and blessed relief from pain, that, when she asked me if I would teach her English, I could not think quickly of a good excuse to say no. I had, quite deliberately, not sought out any students since my arrival on Paros. I had been teaching for over a decade and I felt I needed some respite from the demands which even the best students sometimes make on one's patience. And I had come to live on the island so that I would have time for myself and for the children.

I used to go the Eleni's home along the seafront in Parikia once a week for the English lesson. Although she was twenty-five, she still lived with her parents. It was not acceptable for young, unmarried women to live alone, she told me. Nor was it possible for her, as a member of a respectable bourgeois family, to meet any men on her own; one of her brothers was always sent along as chaperon when she went on a date. There were not too many of those because the poor man's intentions would be questioned by both families if more than half a dozen dates were arranged without any talk of an engagement. As an educated woman with a profitable profession, from a well-off family who could provide a substantial *prika* or dowry, Eleni had many suitors, but she was not attracted to the young men her family approved of. I learned a good deal about the sexual mores of the island during the English lessons with Eleni. I also learned a lot more of the Greek language than Eleni did English during those "lessons".

At the beginning of each session, I tried valiantly to impress on my student that the purpose of the exercise was for her to learn English. That was, after all, why she was paying me. She would nod seriously and bend her dark head over the textbook we were using. But inevitably, after ten or fifteen minutes, she would lose her self-control, her concentration would falter, and she would break breathlessly into Greek to pour out to me the problems she was having with her current secret love affair and to ask me how women conducted their affairs in Ireland. She could not confide the details of her relationships or her problems to her family or friends, she said. Paros is a small island, everyone knows everyone and it would not be safe. As I was an outsider who did not know any of the people in question, beyond recognising some of them in the street, she felt she could safely confide in me and ask my unbiased advice.

Electra, the village midwife, was a close friend of Eleni and she, too, asked me to give her English lessons. I resigned myself to the fact that the word was out. I might as well give in gracefully. I had no reasonable excuse for refusing to give lessons. I was a qualified teacher with a good deal of experience in teaching English as a foreign language and, as far as potential students were concerned, I did not have a job outside the home, so they reckoned I had plenty of time to teach them. Besides, although the cost of living in Greece was a good deal lower than in Ireland, we were spending more than we had budgeted for and the money from the English lessons came in handy.

Like her friend Eleni, Electra was a single woman in her twenties. Her love life was a lot more complicated, however. As she was not from Paros, she did not have the same family constraints as Eleni, so she was free to play the field. Her freedom, however, did not seem to bring her greater happiness or peace of mind. Electra got involved with the wrong types, with married men who had no intention of leaving their wives or returning the *prika* (dowry), or with perennial Don Juans who took up with her in the winter when the tourist girls had left the island. We rarely got ten minutes of any English lesson completed before Electra began recounting her romantic troubles to me in rapid Greek. I would beg her to give me at least the first half-hour to get through a few language exercises. I would refuse to speak any Greek to her. It made no difference whatsoever. She was in a constant state of turmoil and she, too, had nobody else to tell her troubles to. Neither woman felt that they were being well treated by the men they knew. Both of them wanted my advice as an experienced married woman and as a liberated woman. I wondered if I should simply give up on the English lessons and charge for counselling instead.

I was not convinced of the usefulness of any counselling I might offer but I listened to Eleni and Electra as empathetically as I could. They seemed to appreciate that, to find it helpful. As an outsider, it was difficult to give any meaningful advice to them. I found Greek society infuriatingly macho. I was constantly affronted by the way some of the men on the island either made passes at me when my husband was not with me or ignored me when he was, addressing all questions and remarks to him.

I was surprised, in later years, when we were walking down a street together, to find that the male shopkeepers would invariably recognise Rory and would greet him warmly by name. They recognised my existence only when Rory would say, "You remember my wife, Fionnuala, don't you?"

"Oh yes," they would reply, "Kyria Fanny." For that is what I was generally called, because many Greeks find Fionnuala either too difficult to pronounce or inappropriate for a grown woman. The feminine diminutive in Greek is *oula*.

"Why do you have a little daughter called Fiona and you, the mother, are named little Fiona?" they used to puzzle.

I asked a Greek friend to explain this phenomenon of non-recognition to me. "How come these men never fail to recognise Rory and yet never show a flicker of recognition of me? Am I like piece of wallpaper," I asked, "so nondescript I make no impression at all?"

110

"The very opposite," she told me. "It wouldn't be proper for these men to be familiar when your husband is there. They have to pretend not to know you, in case he would be jealous. They feel that they can address you only after your husband has given permission, as it were, by 'introducing' you to them."

Perhaps I took the whole Greek male/female roles and relationships too much to heart. Maybe it is just a game played in warm climates and not to be taken seriously.

Dimitris and Giorgos were my first male students. They were both teachers at the gymnasium, of science and mathematics respectively. They already knew a little English, they said. They'd heard about me from Electra and asked if I would teach them both for the price of a private lesson for one person. Teachers are poorly paid in Greece so I agreed. At least, I thought, with two of them in the class, they are not going to be able to divulge their innermost secrets to me or use me as a counsellor. Not that men were likely to do that anyway, but you never knew. So far, my English lessons had been more in the nature of the confessional or consultations on the psychiatrist's couch. Made wary by the frequent passes made by Greek men of all ages, I was doubly relieved that there would be two of them in the class. We agreed that lessons would take place in their apartment after school twice a week.

With Northern European punctuality, I would turn up at the appointed hour for the lessons, having cycled in from Villa Ariadne in all weathers. They were rarely at the apartment when I arrived. I used to wait in the kafeneion across the road reading a book until they turned up, more often than not, hot and sweaty after a game of football.

"Oh, you are here," they would say vaguely as if I had just happened to be passing by. I started to come ten minutes late. That did not work, either. They either forgot about the lesson entirely or stayed on to play football or drink coffee with the other teachers after school finished, so that when they remembered they had an English lesson, they generally came half-an-hour after lesson time.

"We'll have to find a solution to this problem," I told them.

"What problem?" they asked.

"The problem of time and memory. My time and your memory. For the last three lessons, you have either not turned up at all or have been very late. That means that my time was wasted and that your memory is faulty." I spoke as sternly as I could in Greek, because, as they had only had thirty-minute English lessons for a few weeks, they could not possibly have understood such a mouthful in English.

"You'll have to pay me for lessons one month in advance and, if you have to cancel a lesson, for really serious reasons only, you must let me know the day before and arrange another convenient time."

They looked like chastened schoolboys and I felt like an old schoolmarm. But I did not relent. Lessons took place on time and regularly from then on. We covered the usual beginners' topics: the days of the week, the seasons, food and drink, shopping . . . shopping? They didn't need such vocabulary. They didn't do any shopping. Never? Well . . . only for cigarettes and newspapers. What about food? They went to a taverna for dinner every day. What about breakfast? Coffee in the kafeneion next door to the school.

Dimitris was a tall bearded man of twenty-six who looked like Che Guevara or a younger version of Dinosaki's priestly father. Like many of the teachers at the gymnasium, he was not a native of Paros. He came, in fact,

112

from the island of Lesbos, quite a distance to the north of Paros. There was no direct ferry connection, you had to go to Piraeus, a seven-hour journey, and then take another ferry from there, another ten hours. In effect it took almost two days to get from Paros to Lesbos. Every two or three weeks Dimitris's sixty-seven year old mother travelled from Lesbos to bring her son freshly laundered clothes and her home-made savory dishes and pastries.

"It's a long journey for an elderly woman, why does she do it?" I wanted to know.

"Because she want. Because I am her son," he explained, as if to a stupid child.

"Because she wants to," I corrected automatically.

"She make good food and there is no laundry here on Paros."

"She makes. You must pronounce the 's' in the third person singular." And what I wanted to add was, "Are you not ashamed of yourself? A big fellow like you relying on his elderly mother to wash his clothes and not able to cook for himself. Couldn't you wash your own clothes at least?"

My stunned silence forced him to continue.

"I don't know nothing about the cooking and the clothes-washing. That is the woman's work." Dimitris blew clouds of smoke from his cigarette, like a dragon in front of the maiden.

And Giorgos was no Saint George to come to my rescue. "This is the work of the women in Greece. Here the men are men and the women are women. What about Irish men? They do not do this clothes-washing, this housework?"

I rashly decided to tell the truth, or my personal experience, at any rate. Well, I told them, my husband was at that moment looking after our daughters while making the dinner so that it would be ready for me when I came back from the English lesson.

"He must be strange fellow, is not possible all Irish men are like this." Giorgos looked puzzled, unsure whether he pitied me or my husband more. He should talk to our neighbour, Andreas, about my OFF days. "What about men like us, not married?"

"Well," I tried to tread carefully in a cultural landmine area, "in my father's time Irish men didn't generally do much in the home, but nowadays most young unmarried men are able to look after themselves. My brothers are bachelors, younger than you. My mother taught them how to cook, they can put clothes into a washing-machine and they generally look after themselves."

"And married men, not the ones like your husband?"

"It depends a lot on their background and age," I replied. "Older married men whose wives don't work outside the home don't usually do much housework or child-minding. But younger married men generally share the housework and child-minding with their partners; not fifty-fifty, perhaps, but a good deal of it. You see, most younger wives or partners in Ireland have jobs these days."

"Ah, this is the problem," said Dimitris, with all the satisfaction of someone who had just found the last word in an annoying crossword puzzle. "Women going out to work. They must to stay at the home to look after the childrens and the house." Giorgos vigorously nodded his agreement with this sentiment.

My two students were university graduates and thus, one would assume, reasonably well-educated. During the course of one of our lessons the subject of political life in England came up. Here I ran into another problem.

"The Queen of England rule England," declared Dimitris, as if he were addressing Parliament.

"Well, she is the titular ruler in that she opens sessions at the Houses of Parliament and signs parliamentary bills into law," I demurred, "but the real power and decision-making lies with the democratically elected government."

"You're wrong," shouted Giorgos, "I read in a newspaper that the Queen is head of state. So is the one which rule the country. Is no questions about that!"

Once again I pointed out the need for a subject of a clause or sentence and the English insistence on 's' in the third person singular of verbs in the present tense.

Maybe such certainties as Dimitris's and Giorgos's are the result of a didactic rote-learning education system which Electra told me she had experienced and which Dimitris and Giorgos must also have undergone and were possibly currently perpetuating. We had many more such tussles. They appeared to regard me as a awkward person who was just being difficult for the sake of it. They had very definite opinions on the total rightness of "the struggle for the Irish independence by the IRA". They knew for certain that the Turks were plotting the overthrow of Greece and that "the blacks" were destroying the social fabric of life in England, a country which neither of them had ever visited. There was no discussion or debate with them. Their belief in their own opinions, no matter how ill-informed, was unshakable.

After a while I did not bothering arguing any more. There are some people with whom debate is possible and some with whom it is definitely not. I corrected their grammar and pronunciation mistakes, gave them remedial exercises to do for homework. And murmured, when there was some outrageous remark, "Well, that's your opinion. I don't agree with it, so we'll leave it there, shall we?"

The one good thing was, by dint of having to speak English, in order to argue their points, they learned a great deal more of the language than my two unhappy women students.

As I pedalled back along the seafront and up the hill home to Parosporos, I wondered again at the absolute certainty with which Giorgos and Dimitris pronounced on almost any topic, whether they knew the slightest thing about it or not. What, I would ask myself, had happened to the intellectual heritage of Greece? What had become of the lessons learned from the discourses of Plato, from the debates in the Agora? But, I reminded myself, to be fair, I was dealing here with the opinions of only two young Greek men, not of the whole nation. Better not make any wild statements myself.

When the summer came and the school term finished, Giorgos and Dimitris left Paros to go home for total maternal care. Our lessons did not resume in the autumn. They considered they had learned enough English, Electra told me. They will probably go on leaving out the 's' in the third person present tense of verbs for the rest of their lives. They may even warn their friends never to go to Ireland or get trapped by an Irish woman who might force them to do their own cooking and wash their own shirts.

Despina was married. She had been married to Costas, one of the few hoteliers on the island, for fifteen years, since she was a twenty-year-old Athenian beauty queen.

"He's taken her away from her beauty salon in Athens, away from the sophisticated life she led there," Electra told me when she asked me if I would expand my English lessons to include her uprooted friend.

I agreed to teach the glamorous Despina twice a week in her apartment when Costas was at work and her son,

Manolis, was at school. From the beginning I was strict with my latest student. I was speaking Greek just this once, I told her, in order to explain how the lessons would be structured. The best way to learn a language was to be compelled to understand and speak it. From now on I would only speak to her in English. I understood that she was a beginner, but she was not to worry, it was possible to have lessons totally through English. I was here to teach her English, not to learn Greek myself, I continued firmly in a voice which I hoped would convince her that I meant business. I did not know what Electra had told her about her own English lessons. The rate of her progress would depend on her, on how much effort she was prepared to put into the lessons and the homework. I was sure she would like to make rapid progress, wouldn't she?

She nodded her beautifully-coiffed head and agreed vigorously. She wanted to impress Costas who did not speak much English. And she wanted to be able to read English fashion magazines and to understand English romance films. Relieved that I did not have to become her counsellor, too, I congratulated myself on my assertiveness.

Our uninterrupted English lessons lasted several weeks until, in the middle of one lesson, Despina burst into tears. "Oh, you don't know what it's like," she cried out in Greek, "living on this miserable island, full of donkeys and dust and peasants, when I was used to such a glamorous life in Athens. You can leave here when you like, I'm stuck here, married to that man. I'm only waiting until my son grows up before I leave this backward place."

Her eyelashes were spiders' legs, mascara ran in black rivulets, destroying her immaculately made-up face, her narrow shoulders heaved under the shoulder-pads of her designer jacket.

117

"But you know, Manolis in only six," she went on through her sobs, "how can I wait here all these years for him to grow up? I'll die of boredom! Oh, I'm so miserable. You can't imagine how depressed I am."

"If it's so terrible for you here, why don't you tell Costas how you feel? It may be possible for him to find a job in Athens." I had to say something. She was literally crying on my shoulder.

"Him? Leave Paros? He couldn't tear himself away from his mother, that witch. Who would he run to when we have a row? No, he'll never move. He's like most Greek men, tied to his mother's apron-strings. Nobody else could possibly give them the total adoration they need."

And so it would go on. Some lessons I actually managed to teach Despina something, more often than not she would burst out with her latest woes and demand that I offer some advice, which I most reluctantly gave and to which she never once listened. Yet, when I would see her with Costas and her son in the street at some island event, she looked the perfectly contented wife and mother, looking after the two men in her life. Maybe she needed the luxury of misery to give her life pathos and significance.

Nearly twenty years later she is still on Paros. Her son, Manolis, left the island long ago, first of all to do his military service and later to go to university in Patras. Despina, glamorous as ever, still hangs adoringly on Costas's arm when they attend the increasingly glamorous number of society events on Paros.

The only student who actually came on time, did his homework and seriously applied himself to learning the language, was Damocles. A short, square-shaped man, with plastered-down, ink-black hair like the ace of spades,

Damocles hid behind enormous, black-framed, bottle-bottom glasses. He was in his unfit forties and walked out to the Villa Ariadne three times a week. My daughters loved his lessons because he invariably arrived bearing a large bar of melting chocolate for each of them.

Damocles was born in Alexandria, one of the thousand members of the Greek diaspora who had made Egypt a prosperous place, for themselves at least, in the first half of this century. He spoke Arabic, French, Italian and Greek fluently. He told me that his mother was Italian, his father Greek and that French was the language spoken in his family home in Alexandria. When I knew him first he was making his living as a sort of scribe; many of the old people in the village were either illiterate or unable to deal with official documents. He also taught French privately. Now he wanted to learn English quickly, hence the thrice-weekly lessons. The parents of the children to whom he taught French wanted them to learn the more commercially useful language.

"Mr Chocolate", the children's favourite visitor, would arrive punctually, panting with the exertion of the half-hour walk out from the village. His homework was carefully written out in large, round, even handwriting, each sentence neatly ruled in red. Everything was perfect, he never made a mistake. Which was why I simply could not understand why he would not, or could not, speak a word of un-aided English. He insisted on speaking to me in French. I would force him to repeat the pronunciation of words in English, I would browbeat him into doing exercises in English, but any time that he needed to ask something or did not understand some rule of grammar, he would revert to French. How he could speak four languages and could not manage the relatively easy English language

119

escaped me. Perhaps he was the kind of man who could not bear to lose face in front of a woman, who would perform only when he was convinced that he was competent enough to avoid making mistakes. Whatever the reason, I never heard him converse in English. When I used to meet him sometimes, sitting at the kafeneion at the port, and tried to get him to use his expensive English, he would smile shyly and answer in Greek or French and give Orla and Fiona money to go to the kiosk and buy ice cream.

I never learned much about Damocles's life except that he had been brought up in Egypt and had come to Paros some fifteen years before we met. He never referred to a wife or children, so I assumed that he was unmarried. He was the type of person you felt might regard any personal questions as embarrassing and obtrusive. The only relative Damocles spoke about was his Italian mother, to whom he appeared to have been very attached. He was a bit of a mystery man in a society in which people knew a good deal about each other, if only because many of them were interrelated. Damocles lived in a dusty house with a flaking sun-bleached door of no definite colour at the intersection of two little streets in the maze of Parikia. The faded shutters were always closed so that you never knew whether he was at home. And you never got into his house, either. One time I had to go there to cancel a lesson for some reason. I knocked at the door and waited. There was silence and then I heard frantic scrabbling sounds inside as if someone was desperately trying to remove incriminating evidence before a police raid. After a few moments, Damocles opened the door just a crack so that I could not see anything of the dark room behind him. He blinked in the bright sun. "Ah, Kyria Fanny." He beamed but did not invite me in. No geraniums bloomed on his windowsills. And his house, the leper of the street, had not been whitewashed for years. Neither had the flagstones in the street outside his front door. Damocles camped in his life, a strange, isolated individual, silent in a land of talkative people. Yet he did not appear to me to be a particularly sad person. I thought of him as a benevolent alien on the planet, who lived as best he could in a place he did not really understand.

Reluctant as I had been to get involved in teaching English, I am very glad that I was forced, by that raging toothache, into doing it. For the English lessons gave me an entrée into and an understanding of Parian society that I would not have otherwise had. I could have participated in island festivals and church ceremonies forever, but I would always have been regarded as a higher-rank tourist, a total outsider. By going into people's houses, working with them, listening to their problems, I was able to integrate as much as any foreigner can in any society. And I learned much of the condition and problems of single and married women in Greece, and of the views of young men about life, love and politics. Ironically by giving English lessons, I also greatly improved my comprehension of the Greek language.

Chapter Nine

Summer Madness

The first few tourists of the season were spotted like migratory birds in the *agora* (marketplace) in Parikia at the beginning of May. Ferry boats from Piraeus increased in frequency from the twice weekly winter schedule to several boats each day. Islands to which it was difficult to travel in winter suddenly became accessible again. Cafes, tourist shops and restaurants, closed all winter, were cleaned out and opened for business and the pace of life on the island hotted up. The port became a place of frenzied activity, the nerve centre of the island.

From our house at Parosporos we could hear the ships' sirens announcing their arrival in the bay. I would look out of our kitchen window to see the ferries sailing like plump white ducks around the twin jagged rocks, which we named *The Sisters*, guarding the entrance to the bay of Paros.

Early in the summer season, after a winter during which

123

we had frequently been cut off for a week at a time in bad weather, the sight of a ship passing *The Sisters* and sounding its siren were welcome signs of connection with the outside world.

Anyone who has ever travelled by boat in Greece will know the enormous clamour, the frenetic activity, the shouting, the revving of engines, the demented whistle-blowing and confusing hand signals of the port police and the general debacle which accompanies the passengers and vehicles disembarking and embarking, often at the same time. Overladen trucks, dangerously swaying, plough up the ramp, their horns blaring. Indomitable little old Greek ladies in black carrying cloth-wrapped bundles and lethal parcels weave in and out between the heaving trucks, determined to get on the ship first and to lay claim to at least three seats where they can stretch out full length, blissfully ignoring the seatless tourists, and sleep for the duration of the voyage.

By the beginning of summer, having spent six months without leaving the island, Rory and I were feeling the effects of mild cabin fever and we were ready to take a few boat journeys ourselves. The children, on the other hand, swore they never wanted to get on "a wobbly ship" again. Obviously their experiences of seasick voyages to Crete and Rhodes had made a lasting impression on their young minds. As they were so adamant that they did not want to go on a boat journey, Rory and I tossed a coin to decide which of us would make the first journey off Paros.

Heads, I won. I made plans to go away for two or three days to another island in the Cyclades. But which one? I had already visited Mykonos and Delos years earlier on a student classical tour of Greece. Ios had a reputation for being a hot spot for young tourists. It was full of bars and discotheques, not my favourite place to spend a holiday. Finally, I decided to go to Sifnos. Maybe I would find out whether or not the men were dour. Maybe I had better find out very little about the men. The real reason I wanted to go to Sifnos was that it is called the Potters' Island. All those brown glazed earthenware casseroles, the jugs, the containers yoghurt is still sold in, the water jars, the ceramic braziers that are sold all over Greece, have been produced for hundreds of years on Sifnos.

During the winter I had been busy doing a lot of pottery, something I have always enjoyed. Banging and thumping a lump of clay to get the air out is one of the best ways I know of releasing tension or aggression to a profitable end result – a lovely pliable piece of clay to make into a dish or pot. As I did not have a potter's wheel in Villa Ariadne, I made slab dishes and pinch pots and fired these in a kiln I dug in the garden and filled with sawdust from Manolis's carpentry workshop. The kiln smouldered and smoked for two days and yielded up a crop of wonderful black pots, not impermeable, of course, as they were not glazed. When they cooled, I polished the pots with a smooth stone and the back of a spoon until I produced a shining ebony creation, something like the pueblo pots made in New Mexico. I made table-lamp bases, vases for dried flowers, ashtrays, small jewellery boxes and wall plaques. I also made objects which I called friendship pots. These were pinch pots made in the curve of my hand. While I turned the lump of clay, pinching it between my thumb and fingers, I closed my eyes and thought about the person for whom I was making the pot, a sort of meditation on friendship. Each pot turned out quite different and unique and, I believe, contained something of the spirit of the friend for whom it was to be a present.

Besides wanting to see the potteries of Sifnos, I had another reason for leaving Paros. We lived on a small island surrounded by the great ring of islands that makes up the Cyclades: Syros, Delos, Mykonos, Milos, Naxos, Ios, Santorini, Serifos, Sifnos, Tinos, Amorgos, that enchanting litany which shimmered enticingly across the sea. For months I had had a great urge to get a closer view of one, at least, of these distant beckoning islands.

A third reason for my desire to get away for a short while was the fact that I realised one day that most of my life I had lived and travelled with others, that I had never spent much time alone. I wanted to travel by myself to a place where I knew nobody and see how I would get on. Going on a four-hour boat journey to spend three days alone on Sifnos might not seem that adventurous, but it would do for starters.

Sifnos is not a wealthy island. Flatter and less fertile than Paros, it does not have the volume of tourists that other islands such as Mykonos or Santorini enjoy or endure. Sifnos produces fruit and vegetables and, of course, the pottery for which it is famous. It has suffered the fate of all the islands after the last war in the depopulation of the countryside and of the villages through emigration. In ancient times, however, Sifnos was quite a wealthy island. Its wealth came from its gold and silver mines, now long gone, either destroyed by volcanos or else worked out. As usual in Greece, there is a legend to explain historical events. The destruction of the mines of Sifnos, according to Pausanias, was brought about by an angry Apollo. It was the tradition to give the god an annual gift of a golden egg. One year, however, the greedy islanders tried to deceive the god by presenting him with a gilded egg. He was so angered by their deceit that he destroyed the source of their gold. Another Golden Goose moral tale.

The little ship *Megalohori* landed at Kamares on the west coast of Sifnos. From there I took a bus that met the ferry up the steep, twisting road to Artemona, the island capital, situated on the spine of the island and looking down on the sea about forty minutes walk away. It was too far from the sea. I knew exactly where I wanted to stay: in an upstairs room directly overlooking the sea. So I left Artemona and took the next bus down to the sea at Castro, the old capital of the island.

As the name implies, Castro is a defensive site. It is built on a hill over the sea and protected by a fourteenth-century wall. Tall Venetian houses built into the wall face across the sea to Paros, now, in turn, a distant, shimmering haze of rock. Layers of streets connect at different levels with footbridges across the streets below. The walls of Castro were built by the Venetian Corognon family and the whole village has something of the feel of the Crusades about it. You could imagine people running in panic through the streets, clutching their children and carrying their valuables in their arms, desperate to escape the ravaging pirates. The labyrinthine streets of so many Greek villages might have been built to confuse pirates or any other invaders and still manage to confuse thousands of tourists who get lost every summer.

"Didn't we see that church before, dear?"

"No, darling, it was a different church, totally different, surely you remember?"

"Well, dear, all I can say is that you're the one who's supposed to be leading us through this bloody village and you haven't managed to find the way out yet. And we've been here for an hour. And it's bloody hot. And I'm sure that we're just going round in circles. This place is a maze."

Having walked around Castro in a few circles myself searching for my upstairs room, I discovered that, as the season in Sifnos had not yet started, there were no rooms to rent in the village. An old woman with no teeth and the enchanting smile of a young baby directed me to Faro, the next village, about half-an-hour's walk along a cliff path. There I found a small picture-postcard fishing village with rooms to let right over the harbour.

From the rickety wooden balcony of my room I could see orange, blue, and yellow fishing caiques bobbing in the clear water below. Fishermen in old trousers and straw hats whistled and shouted to one another as they mended tears in their nets or sloshed buckets of water over the decks of their salty boats. A high ceiling, a painted wooden floor, an iron bedstead, clean white sheets, a speckled mirror, a cheap rather gaudy icon of St Nicholas, the patron saint of sailors, a small, blue, wooden table at the window, a Van Gogh chair – a perfect place to think and to write, to be alone. And all for one hundred and twenty drachmas, about two pounds, a night.

Next morning I was up before dawn like a nun at matins. I watched the sun paint a faint streak of pale yellow along the watery horizon. I enjoyed every minute of that daybreak as if it were the very first I had ever seen. Quiet and calming, the start of a day when everything is possible. Before breakfast I swam across the stilly bay, hardly daring to disturb the mirrored surface of the sea. Breakfast was a bowl of thick home-made yoghurt with honey, nuts and apricots in the only kafeneion which was open and where the owner called me *kukla* (doll) and I told him firmly that my husband would be joining me soon.

For the entire day I sat writing at my table by the window, relishing the wonderful peace of being alone; no children, no husband, no expectations. By the evening I had come to the conclusion that a spell in a convent might be a very good idea as I had managed to finish a short story on which I had laboured for weeks. When I finally looked at my watch, I was astonished to discover that it was half-past five. Time for another swim before dinner.

When I got back to the beach after my swim two fair-skinned girls were playing chess on a beach-mat where I had left my towel. Their skin tone and colouring told me they were probably Irish and when they spoke, I was proved correct. Siobhan and Clare were architectural students having a break just after their final exams. They were camping in a field behind the beach just for the night and were leaving Sifnos the following day.

At dinner we discovered, as is almost inevitable when Irish people meet abroad, that we had friends and acquaintances in common. Perhaps this is due to the small size of our country, or maybe it is because, traditionally, families are quite large, so everyone knows someone you went to school or college with, or who knows your brothers, sisters or cousins. I have met people who knew school friends of mine from Belfast in an Indian store in remotest Zambia. In India, Rory and I went into a faded ex-colonial restaurant in Poona and sat down next to a man in a beige suit and a woman in a twinset and pearls and tightly permed hair – both from Rory's English seminar group at Trinity – now missionaries to the Hindus.

Bumping into people you know or who know you in all parts of the world is both reassuring – we are never alone – and unsettling – you cannot move without being observed.

Next morning I was woken before dawn by a loud

banging of shutters and the sound of wind howling like a wolf along the harbour wall. A gale-force wind was blowing. No caiques had gone out the night before and they were now tossing about in the port like boats in a cartoon film.

Around midday I saw the two Irish girls struggle off the Artemona bus with their rucksacks. They had been down to Kamares to catch a ferry to Piraeus and had been told that, as force 8 to 9 gale-force winds had been forecast for the next three days, it was most unlikely that they would be able to get off the island until after that. They were upset as they would miss their charter flight to London and had already spent most of their money.

This is where knowing people comes in useful. I lent them what money I could spare, so that at least they had enough to survive on until their ferry sailed.

I could not phone Rory to let him know that I was going to be delayed for three days because nobody we knew had a phone. At that time in Paros a phone was a treasure very few people possessed; there seemed to be only a few lines available on the whole island. No point writing a letter either as the post went by ferry. So all I could do was hope that when he and the children turned up the next day to meet the boat I was supposed to be on, the port police would tell him that no ferries could sail from Sifnos.

There is something exhilarating about lack of choice. I think there is a Zen Buddhist saying, "Freedom is lack of choice." Certainly, not being able to get off Sifnos allowed me to relax completely, to take whatever turned up and to go with the flow of life. In the mornings I wrote at my window and in the afternoons I forgot about my need to be alone. We three marooned Irish women explored most of Sifnos, mainly on foot. We came across wonderful, remote

130

monasteries perched like eagles' nests on spectacular cliffs over the sea or wedged into clefts in the sides of mountains. We ate our shepherd's lunch of bread, cheese and olives and drank bottles of dry red wine in flowering meadows loud with bees. We sang Irish rebel songs and we told stories about people we knew and places we had been.

At a festival in the monastery of Chrissi Pigi, the Golden Well, built into the side of a cliff at the end of a long thin peninsula, the monks and local villagers provided an open house, with food, wine and dancing for everyone who came. Such unexpected festivities and such casual hospitality to strangers are part of the surviving charm of Greece.

When the wind abated a little, word came to Faro that the ferry for Piraeus would leave. My two companions said goodbye and I was on my own again. The sea was still too rough for the smaller ferry to Paros, so I had no choice but to stay where I was and enjoy the peace.

In the five days I had spent walking around the island I was disappointed that I had not come across any potteries. However, as I strolled along the waterfront at Faro after my compatriots had left, I saw smoke rising from the chimney of an odd-shaped structure on the hill behind the shore. I climbed up to have a look and found Vasilis, the only remaining potter on that side of the island. He was a short man of about sixty with muscular brown arms and legs and thick grey hair. His black piratical moustache, which must have been dyed, gave him a rakish air which belied his gentle hesitant voice and manner. He was wearing an old pair of trousers rolled up to the knee and a mud-spattered vest that was once white. His small eyes were dark and shaded and his handshake was very firm.

For the next five days I worked with Vasilis, learning

131

how to make the traditional earthenware pots for which Sifnos is famous. *Tsoukalia*, which are ovenproof casserole dishes, small Greek coffee cups, terracotta water containers, we made them all. His workshop was a low, windowless room in a traditional peasant house. Rows of pots were stacked to dry on sagging wooden shelves which lined the walls of the workshop. And all along the floor were more pots waiting to be glazed and decorated before being fired in the kiln. The light came from the open door and his foot-propelled potter's wheel was set into the earthen floor just inside the door. Sitting there on a low stool in my bare feet, kicking the wheel and throwing pots, I could look out over the back of the rippling bay to the misty island of Paros beyond and I could imagine my round-eyed Fiona asking every morning, "When is Mammy coming back?" And her father reassuring her that Mammy would come back when the wind stopped blowing so hard and the ship could sail from Sifnos.

Vasilis never weighed the clay or measured the pots he made. *"Na kanome tsoukalia,"* (Let us make tsoukalia) he would say, breaking off two lumps of equal size from the mass of soggy clay in the trough where it was prepared. After kneading them well, he would take one of the lumps and throw a pot. The second ball of clay would be used as a gauge for all subsequent pots, so that each one was identical in height and diameter. He had a rota: some days he made nothing but *tsoukalia* all day, the next day it might be water jugs; the third day braziers.

Vasilis could not understand my need to try something different once in a while, to vary the shape of the handles, for instance. *"Yiati?"* he would protest. His grandfather and father had been making *tsoukalia* in that way, with those handles, all their lives. That is how he had been taught to do it and that is how he would go on making all his pots, exactly according to tradition.

He and his wife had not had any children. That made him sad because he had no son to whom he could pass on his skills. And now it was far too late because Nectaria was fifty. He sighed. Of course, if he had a younger wife, it would still be possible for him to have a son. It was a mistake to marry late in life and then to marry a woman not much younger than oneself. His nephews had emigrated to Athens and as far away as Australia, so they would not be carrying on the potters' trade. When he retired in ten years or so, that would be the end of a family dynasty of potters which stretched back one hundred and fifty years.

It was a hard life, he told me, but satisfying. He did everything himself. He dug and prepared the clay, made and glazed the pots and cut the wood to fire his three-chambered kiln, built by his grandfather. From beginning to end the pots were Vasilis. He had a firing once a week and his pots were distributed and sold all over Greece.

The little house at Faro had neither electricity nor running water. Water for the pottery came from a well on the terrace. Vasilis worked in the Faro workshop for eight months of the year and spent the winter months, when the days were too short and there was not enough light, in Artemona with his wife. Nectaria, he complained, was only interested in cooking and gossiping, not at all in making pots and she would not live with him in Faro. Too quiet, according to her, and too far from the church.

She came to visit him on the Sunday afternoon bus, a well-upholstered woman, about a head taller than Vasilis, with quick sharp eyes and grey-black hair dragooned by steel clips into a tight bun. Nectaria looked the indefinite age of so many Greek women over thirty, anywhere between forty and sixty. She greeted me cooly, her natural Greek hospitality tempered by suspicion.

Vasilis had never before met a woman who was could throw pots. "Oh," I told him, "I'm not unusual. There are lots of women potters in Ireland. Surely there are some in Greece, too."

"But you're good," he flattered me. "Even if you want to change the Sifnos way of making *tsoukalia*."

It did not occur to me that Vasilis might have had any ulterior motives in inviting a foreign woman half his age to work with him in the pottery. I should not have underestimated the irrepressible vanity and the underlying macho nature of so many Greek males, regardless of age or decrepitude. His first few shy sly suggestions I dismissed, thinking I had misunderstood him. I told myself that my Greek really was pretty weak. One day, however, when I arrived to start the day's work, he grabbed me around the waist and embraced me. Pulling away from his sinewy arms, I laughed foolishly, as if it was I who had offended and told him not to be silly.

I have never known what to do at such times. I seem to get this frozen smile on my face, my tongue deserts me, and I try to pretend that nothing has happened, that nothing was meant, really. I do not feel in the least flattered, rather I feel annoyed by what I regard as unnecessary juvenile interruptions to what might have been an interesting conversation or a pleasant acquaintance. My first reaction is to try to ignore the pass and to hope that the silly man will get the message fast so that I will not have to put him down.

I thought Vasilis had got my message. He let me go and busied himself wedging a great lump of clay. I varied the shape of the handles on a *tsoukali* I was making and he said nothing.

I was wrong. At lunch-time, Vasilis came up behind me where I sat at the wheel and whispered something in my ear. "I can't understand what you are saying," I said, not really wishing to have him raise his voice and repeat what I thought he had said.

"We will have our siesta now," he said loudly. "Together." In case I misunderstood.

Usually he had his siesta somewhere in the dim recesses of the workshop while I went for a swim and a sunbathe on the beach. Before I could splutter a reply, he reminded me that his wife only came down from Artemona on Sundays so we would be quite safe. I reminded that I was happily, very happily, married, that I had two children and that he, too, was married. I should also have pointed out to him that he was old enough to be my father.

He waved these slight impediments aside. "Bah, we're not talking about wives and husbands or children. We're only talking about a little siesta."

I had to do my ice-maiden act. I stood up from the wheel, wiped my dirty hands on my T-shirt and glared down at him.

"I enjoy working here in the pottery with you," I told him, "and I'm learning a lot. But if you don't stop doing and saying such stupid things, I won't come again. Do you understand?"

At least that is the gist of what I told him in ungrammatical Greek. He understood.

"Irish women are so cold," he muttered, "it must be all that rain."

Although the weather at Faro was sunny and relatively calm, the storms continued at sea and no ferries left for

135

Paros, so I spent the next three days in Vasilis's workshop. We stacked the kiln and fired a week's hard work. We worked in near silence. Vasilis had lost the need to impress me. I concentrated on making perfect pots and experimented with more variations on the *tsoukalia* theme, which I told Vasilis I would pay for and keep myself.

Eighteen years later I returned to Sifnos and to Faro. I was relieved and delighted to find that nothing had changed very much in the village. The owner of the kafeneion was stooped with age and called me *kyria* and not *kukla*, so some things had changed. I searched the hill above the beach, looking for smoke rising from a kiln. The sky was clear. Nonetheless, I climbed up to the pottery and, to my surprise, found the door of the workshop open. There, sitting in leaden silence at an oilcloth-covered table where the wheel used to be, eating a lunch of tomatoes, bread and olives, were Vasilis and Nectaria. Vasilis had developed a paunch and his pirate's moustache was straggly and grey. Nectaria was even plumper than she had been, except for her face which was like a hatchet in profile. The sagging shelves were empty of pots and there was a brass double bed where the clay-trough had been. Black dresses hung on nails behind the door and women's shoes lay in an untidy pile under the bed. Nectaria obviously stayed longer than Sunday afternoons. A row of bikinis hung out to dry on a clothes-line stretched across the terrace between the old workshop and the kiln.

"Do you remember me, the Irish woman who worked with you here many years ago?" I asked the blinking old man. I thought I caught just a hint of a sheepish look in his eyes when he looked at me and remembered. Nectaria looked stolidly through me. There had obviously been

136

other foreign women in the intervening years. Maybe some of them were more obliging than the cold Irish one. I wondered whether Vasilis had ever changed his mind about Irish women. Nectaria did not invite me to join them for lunch.

Vasilis took me outside to show me what he had done with the kiln. It had been extended and converted into three rooms. He had retired years before and he made his living now by renting rooms to tourists in the summer. Many Italian and German girls had stayed there, he told me, very pretty, very nice.

Before I left, I took a photograph of the old couple standing outside their summer house with the line of drying bikinis, like Buddhist prayer flags, flapping behind them.

On the eleventh day the wind finally abated and the ferryboat sailed for Paros. My forced sojourn on Sifnos had been fruitful. I had completed two short stories and made a boxful of pots, jugs and plates which Vasilis carefully wrapped up in straw and put into a cardboard box tied up with agricultural twine. I had thoroughly enjoyed being on my own but was very much looking forward to being reunited with Rory and the children.

Orla and Fiona were waiting for me as the ferry docked in Parikia. There was no sign of my beloved husband. Sheila, our dish-washing philosopher friend, was holding the girls' hands. "He's gone fishing," she announced, "with Leonardo, on his caique. They couldn't wait any longer. Left yesterday. Said to tell you he'll be back in a week or so."

So it was my turn to take over the solo parenting of our two children. Did they wonder why one parent left the island just before the other arrived home? I do not know. They did not ask. Fiona said, "The big wind stopped you coming home, didn't it, Mammy? But it's gone now." And Orla told me, "Daddy bought us loads of sweets and ice cream." Children are marvellous at adapting to whatever fate their parents inflict on them.

Costas worked in the post office and spent a lot of his time also around the church of Zoodochos Pigi. He seemed to be a sort of voluntary church warder. Often on my way past the church to Dinosaki's, I used to see his lanky frame standing at the church porch where he sold candles to the worshippers. We nicknamed him "Brylcreem" because of the amount of the stuff he plastered on his black hair. He looked like a veritable Uriah Heep of unctuousness.

Every few days we called to the post office to collect our mail from the poste restante. Dimitris, the manager, Maria, the woman who sorted the letters, Petros, the postman and Costas all knew us and often gave sweets to the children, as so many Greeks like to do. A few days after Rory's departure on his caique, I went to the post office hoping to find lovely letters from home. Costas gave a bar of chocolate to the children and asked me, "And your husband, where is he? I haven't seen him for a few days."

"Oh, he's gone fishing with Leonardo," I informed him brightly. "He'll be away for about a week."

There were several letters for us in the *beta* pigeon hole. As he handed them to me Costas asked casually, "Have you ever been to Mykonos?"

"Yes," I replied, "but it was a long time ago, when I was a student."

"Would you like to go again?"

"Yes, I'll probably go back there sometime. I love the architecture of the town."

He leaned forward over the counter. I could see a faint white bald spot on the top of his head under the lid of oiled hair. "I could arrange that for you. I have friends who own boats that go there. You won't have to pay anything. I can arrange everything."

"That would be great."

Why not? Mykonos is only about two hours from Paros, an easy day-trip.

"Well, then, let me know when you want to go." He uncoiled like a cobra from the counter and straightened himself up to deal with the next customer.

I told the children that we might be going away just for a day on a boat to another lovely island. I had to persuade them that the journey would be very different to the long voyages they had had to endure the previous autumn. So, a few days later I told Costas that the children and I were ready to go to Mykonos the next day.

"I'm not sure whether that's OK or not. Maybe later. Please check with me tomorrow." He seemed a bit put out about something.

As the weather was very calm and ferries were leaving Paros every day for Mykonos, I could not understand what was bothering Costas. The next morning I went into the post office to check with him. He hummed and hawed, running his thin fingers through the oily Brylcreem.

"What's the problem, Costas?" I asked. "The weather's fine and the boats go every day. Does your friend no longer own the boat?"

"That's not the problem," he muttered looking down at his shining shoes.

"Then, what is it?" I persisted.

"I'm not free to go today. I can't get away for a few days."

Not again! Even this starched paragon, this pillar of the church, this handwringing verger was affected by the machismo which seems to be endemic in the southern Mediterranean. He, too, had to try to make *kamaki*. The fact that he knew my husband and children seemed to make no difference. The husband was away and the chance was there. I began to understand the plight of the young widow in the film *Zorba the Greek* and I felt an immense empathy with the legendary Penelope.

It was not expensive to go to Mykonos. I took the children there for the day, they were not seasick, and we enjoyed the trip. Costas resumed his church-warden manners when he met me in the street or served me in the post office. He is another of those men who always recognise Rory and seems to be a trifle vague as to my identity until Rory says, "Costas, you must remember my wife, Fionnuala."

Two weeks after he had left Paros, a very salty, unshaven, Moby Dick character rolled in the door of Villa Ariadne and threw a large, dripping plastic bag smelling of fish on the table. "The rest are in the morgue," he said wearily.

"The rest of what, who?" I screamed.

"The fish, what do you think? We don't have a fridge here, so I've left kilos of fish in the morgue." Rory was so exhausted that he could give no further explanation until he woke late that evening. It seemed that part of his wages as one of Leonardo's crew was in kind. The fish which they had not sold was divided among the crew. Rory's share amounted to about ten kilos of assorted fish. Electra, my love-sick student, who worked in the clinic, had bumped into him as he struggled past the port kafeneion under his fishy booty and had offered to help. Apparently there was a large fridge in the clinic which served as a morgue. As it was conveniently empty, she had suggested it as a solution to Rory's fish-storage problem.

"Well, I hope nobody dies suddenly or no tourist gets killed on a motor-bike in the next few days," I said, making plans to put fish on the menu for a series of dinner parties. "Otherwise we'll have a lot of stinking fish on our hands and the corpses will go to their graves with the smell of fish on them."

By the end of the week during which, mercifully, nobody had been inconsiderate enough to die, the "morgue" was emptied of its strong-smelling contents. Rory managed to get rid of the ingrained salt from his skin and clothes and shaved off his Captain Ahab beard.

The experience of living for a few weeks on a traditional caique with the island fishermen made such an impression on Rory that he wrote a poem entitled "Leonardo's Crew", which he included in his second collection, *The Walking Wounded*. This is the first verse of the poem.

The serrated currents sawed the boat
Across the shoulderblade of bay again.
This time the sounder drew a plain and gulf
Where Leonardo knew to lay his labyrinth
Of nets already stacked like hives along the deck.
So close to life are the tough trades of death
We flatter them with talk of purity. Old
Andreas dealt the nets like cards across the stern.

Life on Paros is full of rich experience, of meeting passing travellers, of easy connections. Like a magnet, Paros attracts many interesting people and, because of the casual, unpretentious atmosphere of the place, it is very easy to make connections. Quite often while shopping in the *agora* or drinking an ouzo at Dinosaki's we would meet strangers who had just arrived on the island. Many's the time either Rory or myself would turn up at Villa Ariadne with an American, Irish or English newcomer in tow. We invited them for lunch, they had stories to tell and the conversation flowed with the farmers' wine.

There was a big difference, however, between the low and high summer season. As the June days grew sunnier and more and more ships deposited their cargoes of tourists, it became virtually impossible to connect with new people. There were simply too many of them. Parikia and Naoussa, the main tourist villages, became claustrophobic. It seemed to us that the population of the island increased a hundred-fold. The residents of Paros, Greek and foreign alike, were overwhelmed by the tidal wave of tourists. We changed our daily habits, went into the village to go to the bank and to do the shopping early in the morning so as to avoid the queues and crowded streets. The shopkeepers became bad-tempered and a few of them started to cheat on their weights and prices. It was impossible to get served in the tavernas and kafeneions. We stayed at home more and entertained ourselves at private parties and dinners. We stayed out of town and out of the way.

My mother was a widow, as were Rory's mother and the aunt with whom she lived in Belfast. All three wrote to say that they missed their granddaughters and would really love to see us all. So we invited them to Paros for a holiday. We did not know that they were going to book three-month return tickets. As Villa Ariadne had one bedroom and bunk beds in the hall and was a good distance out of Parikia, we found them an apartment to rent in the village with a balcony overlooking the sea.

It is not perhaps the best idea to have your parents living very close to you on a small island for a long period. Not that there were any personal difficulties. The problems were caused by the alternative lifestyles of many of our friends on Paros and by their preferred bathing attire. "The grannies," as everyone we knew on the island called them, did not approve of people who were not married living together. "And where is she from? And what does he do? And are they married?"

They certainly did not approve of nudism on the beaches. "Fionnuala, go over and tell that man to put bathing trunks on. Tell him there are young children around. It's shocking," one of them would command me.

"I don't think the children have noticed," I would reply, "they're used to it. Anyway, I know that man and I don't think he would take too kindly to being told to put on swimming trunks."

"You know that man! Who is he? It really is a disgrace! And it's against the law. Look at the signs all over the place."

The grannies fitted into Greek society very well. They attended many services at the nearby church. They participated in baptisms and weddings and were on nodding terms with the priests and with Brylcreem. Dinosaki approved of them and gave them his special service. He appreciated people who attended church services in the church where his father had been a priest.

Orla and Fiona revelled in the undivided attentions of three grandmothers, for Rory's aunt was regarded by all of us as another grandmother. The children's consumption of ice cream and *karameles* increased alarmingly and I warned the indulgent suppliers that I was not going to be responsible for any dental bills for the next year.

143

We seemed to spend a good deal of the summer meeting friends who arrived to visit us on the ferry from Piraeus and seeing them off again two or three weeks later. In the intervening weeks we showed off our island as proudly as if we were native Parians. We took our friends to all the scenic places, to the best beaches and tavernas. We introduced them to Paros wine, we picnicked and swam. When it was simply too hot to go anywhere, we spent long, drowsy afternoons sitting in deckchairs under the shade of the eucalyptus tree on the terrace of Villa Ariadne with a plate of luscious red watermelon and a jug of home-made lemonade to keep us cool.

The summer months were one long holiday for us and the children were happy to be the centre of so much attention. However, there was not enough time or quiet to do much reading, writing, weaving, pottery or philosophy. By the time our last guests had left at the beginning of September, when the grapes were ready for picking, we were ready to return to a more leisurely and a more productive lifestyle and to renew the quiet Parian way of living after the summer madness.

Chapter Ten

To School Through the Agora

After a summer of idleness, we had to bestir ourselves to enrol Orla in school at the beginning of September. You would think that children would pick up a language without effort, merely by living in the country where the language was spoken. It is not so. Orla and Fiona had been almost one year in Greece and they did not speak more than a few words. *Pagota* (ice cream), *karameles* (sweets) and *parakalo* (please) were their favourites. They were surrounded by English at home, their friends spoke it and thus had not been forced to speak Greek.

Kyrios Roussos, the headmaster of the *demotikon* in Parikia, was a little reluctant to take our daughter into the first class of his school because she spoke hardly any Greek and there was no provision in the school for the teaching of non-native speakers. No teacher in the school, including himself, spoke any English and he thought it would be hard going for our six-year-old daughter. But we persisted.

Children need the socialisation aspect of school, we argued, and we also wanted our children to be able to communicate in Greek and to make friends among the local children. We wanted them to learn about the culture of the community among whom we were living. And the only way that could happen would be for them to attend the *demotikon*.

Finally, he agreed to enrol Orla in the *proti taxi* or first class. Fiona was still only three years of age and would not be able to go the kindergarten until she was four. We were to provide Orla with a uniform and make sure that she did her homework. The uniform for Greek state schools seems to be standard all over the country. At that time it consisted of a marine blue dress, the colour of the Greek flag, with a detachable white collar for girls and blue shorts and white shirts for boys.

The design of primary schools also seems to be standard throughout Greece. They are long, single-storied neo-classical buildings with high ceilings, tall windows and pillared porticos. The *demotikon* in Parikia is situated in the heart of the village, at the far end of the *agora*, beside the Ekatonpyliani church. It is surrounded by a dappled playground, shaded by eucalyptus and tamarisk trees.

On her first day in her new school the whole family accompanied Orla right up to the door of her classroom. As she had already been at school for a year in Ireland and had enjoyed the experience, she did not appear to be nervous or to suffer from first-day-at-school-nerves. Of course, this time it would be different as she was going into a classroom where none of the children spoke her language, where she could not communicate with anyone, not even the teacher.

That very first day when we took the unsuspecting

child into the classroom where she was to spend the next year, my heart tumbled like a stone in a well when I saw the blank, putty-coloured walls. No charts, posters, pictures, nothing colourful, nothing at all for the children to look at or to be stimulated by. Maybe, it's because they took everything down at the end of last term, I tried to reassure myself. Rory looked equally disturbed. I glanced around the classroom. On a high shelf, out of reach of the tiny pupils, were stacked piles of tattered readers. There was no evidence of art or craft supplies, no maps, no library books, none of the many teaching aids which filled classrooms in Ireland. The walls were bare and I could see no cupboards which might contain such materials and aids. The only furniture was the rows of wooden desks and chairs and the dais on which the teacher sat. On a bright, sunny, early autumn day the classroom was chillingly dull. Again I told myself that it was only the first day of term, that the colourful charts and visual aids, the counting blocks, the art supplies were most probably in storage and would be brought out during the course of the day. Still, the visual desert did not say much for the teacher's preparation of the classroom to welcome children on their first day at school.

On the stroke of half past eight the class teacher arrived, a short, plump woman of around forty with sculpted black hair and tight lips. Ignoring the group of parents crowding the doorway, she segregated off the children like a clever sheepdog and closed the classroom door firmly. There was no question of our being allowed to stay in the classroom with the child for a short while until she got used to her surroundings. The other parents seemed to accept the situation and so Rory and I had no choice but to leave. Before I left I tried to peer through the dirty windows to see what had happened to Orla. I saw a milling crowd of small children in blue and the teacher shoving some of them into seats. Orla's was standing near the door and her bewildered face was like a rebuke.

Neither Rory nor I could speak on the way home. I had a painful lump in my throat and a sense of foreboding in my heart. I could sense Rory's unease and his questioning whether we had done the right thing in enrolling Orla in the *demolikon*. Fiona, chewing a sweet she had wheedled from Manolis, the grocer, sat on the motor-bike between us, lost in the sticky dreams of three-year-olds.

Orla was more than bewildered when I called to collect her at midday. She was a sad-eyed, subdued little girl, totally unlike her normal bubbly self.

"What does *'figi mure'* mean?" she asked me on the way home.

I only knew that *figi* was the imperative form of the verb to go. I had to ask Maria the meaning of *mure*.

"It isn't a very nice word," she told me, "it means a stupid person."

I did not translate for Orla.

The next day Rory took her to school. When he had finished the shopping, he went round the back of the school to the wall beside the playground where he could see the children playing at break-time, without being seen by them.

"Orla was just sitting by herself on a bench outside the classroom window. Nobody talked to her, nobody included her in their games. She seemed dazed," he told me, a catch in his voice.

On the third day I decided to go and see Kyria Dolkas to ask how Orla was getting on.

"Yiati clei?" she demanded.

148

"I'm sorry, Kyria, I don't understand the word *clei*," I replied.

She wiped her eyes and made a sniffing sound. "*Clei, clei,*" she repeated.

"Ah, why does she cry? I don't know why," I replied, almost crying myself. "I'll ask her."

Orla told me that she cried because when she went into the classroom every morning and sat at the desk where she had been the day before, other children came up and roughly pushed her out of her seat, so that she did not know where to sit or where to go. She could not understand what they were saying, they always said the same thing: *Figi mure.* She stood at the back of the classroom until everyone had sat down and then sat in whatever seat was left empty. The teacher did not help her or say anything to the children who pushed her.

"Do those children who push you do the same to other girls or boys?" I asked the white-faced child.

"Oh yes," she said, "but they do it more often to me and I don't know what to do 'cos they can't understand me and I don't know what they're saying."

"But surely the teacher has written all the children's names on their desks so they can go to the same place every day?"

"No, there aren't any names on the desks and nobody has a place of their own. There's a big fight every morning to get seats and the boys are very rough," she sobbed.

"My daughter tells me that she cries because other children push her out of the seat she is sitting in and she doesn't know where to go. She says that nobody has his or her own place and that everyone fights for a seat. She says that there is a lot of upset because of this every morning."

149

Kyria Dolkas glared at me from behind her thick glasses and I prayed that my poor daughter would not be further victimised, but I just could not bear to see my child so unhappy. So, taking a deep breath, I continued, in a very conciliatory voice and as diplomatically as I could, "I wonder if you would consider giving each child their own seat, maybe write their names on the desks, so that they'd always know where to go and they'd feel secure?" I had spent a considerable time with my dictionary the evening before.

"I don't care what they do in schools in your country," Kyria Dolkas snapped, "you're in Greece now. Here we do things our way."

I felt like a spanked child, helpless and furious.

If things did not improve, we would have to consider removing our daughter from the school, something we were reluctant to do. However, two days later when I took Orla into her classroom there were large name-labels on each desk and all the children were sitting peacefully in their places.

The walls of the classroom never became colourful or stimulating. As the year progressed some charts showing the alphabet, many pictures of the saints and a map of Greece went up on the wall. The children's artwork consisted of colouring in outlines of houses or animals stamped on thin cheap paper. These dull sheets were pinned in regimented and identical rows along the wall. There was no nature study, no physical education or music taught, but there was a heavy diet of religion. Every day started with prayers at school assembly, followed, in Orla's class at any rate, by another ten minutes of prayers. In the course of the morning there would be another half-hour lecture on the saint of the day or some other religious topic. Kyria Dolkas seemed to be a religious fanatic and every lesson was punctuated with prayers. Orla soon knew every saint in the orthodox calendar.

Rory and I often debated the wisdom of our decision to send our child to that school. We did not wish to condemn the entire Greek education system because our daughter was experiencing an unenlightened, nineteenth-century style education in a particular village school, with a particular teacher. We argued that one could not make judgements based on one individual experience, that maybe Orla was just unlucky in that her teacher was unimaginative, over-zealous in the religious department and resistant to modern teaching methods and that the rest of the teachers in the school were fine. However, we could not stand by and do nothing. At the same time we did not want to cause the child more problems by in any way appearing too critical of the teacher or of the type of education Orla had to endure at the hands of Kyria Dolkas. Conscious of the fact that we were foreigners and had little right to protest about the way the education system was run, we went to see the headmaster to explain some of our concerns to him. He was very understanding. Orla's teacher, he told us, was indeed old-fashioned in her approach. She was a very religious person who was concerned about the decline in moral standards in modern Greece and she wanted all her pupils to know their religion thoroughly. However, he assured us, she was very conscientious, a good teacher of the basic subjects and, though strict and lacking in humour, she was not cruel or unkind. He promised to have a word with her about the special needs of a foreign child who was just learning the language and he was sure she would try to ensure that Orla was made more welcome by the other children and included in their games. So we decided to leave Orla in the school for a while and to take her away if the situation became unbearable for her.

Within three months Orla was practically fluent in Greek. She could read and write the language as well as any Greek child of her age and she was an expert on saints. She announced every morning at breakfast which saint had a feast-day that day. She told us that she did not cry any more and that the teacher was nicer to her.

But, when Rory or I sneaked round the back of the school to watch the children at break time, we used to see her playing alone, her blonde curly head bent over a little red toy car she took to school with her every day.

We made up for the lack of artistic outlet in school by having art and craft lessons at home as well as drama and nature-study sessions. We also continued her English and Irish reading lessons and we told more stories at bedtime. We hoped we were doing the right thing. The brave child never complained, but it was heartbreaking for us to watch the solitary little figure pushing her red car around the edges of the playground while the other children played noisy games from which she was excluded.

Orla was a gentle child, not very shy but not assertive either. If another child pushed her, she did not push back, nor did she go running to adults to complain about being bullied. She just tried to get on with her life quietly in her day-dreaming way. She hated shouting and fighting and would go off by herself when there was any conflict. Perhaps the reason the little Greek children did not include her in their games, besides the fact that in the beginning she did not speak Greek, was that her diffidence and self-reliance might have led them to think she was aloof. Still, Rory and I felt that it was the teacher's role to ensure that her little foreign pupil was made welcome in the school. She could have easily arranged for some kind child to play with Orla and encouraged the others to include her in the playground games. Certainly, she should have put a stop to the shouting of *Figi mure* at Orla, or at any other child. Children in any society can easily learn to become xenophiles instead of xenophobes.

As time went on, Theothisksti, another shy little blonde girl, who lived near the Wheelers, began to play with Orla and we were delighted to see our daughter's face assume its familiar cheerful smile again.

One of the positive results of Orla's going to the village school was a great push forward in my Greek studies. Name-days forced me to shift off the linguistic plateau where I had lodged for months. Children's name-days are celebrated in Greece in much the same way as children's birthdays are in Ireland. Orla was invited to all the name-day parties, by children who never spoke to her or played with her in school. I was wearing jeans and a sweater when I dropped Orla off at her first party at some Dimitris's or Maria's house. On entering the sitting-room, I was surprised to see all the other mothers sitting around on chairs and sofas, dressed to the nines, drinking coffee and eating pastries. The hostess invited me to stay and expressed clicking disappointment when I explained that I could not as I had to do the shopping and that, in any case, I had not understood that parents also attended children's parties.

After that I had to dress up and spend hours chatting to the other mothers at the name-day parties. Fathers were never expected to take the children or to attend the parties. More women's work. As my grasp of the language improved, I was acquainted with the island gossip and began to feel that I was at last beginning to be part of the wider island community. More people greeted me on the street and in the shops now that I was the mother of a child in the *proti taxi*. Thus we were accepted as part of the island society in a way that would not have happened had we not had a child at school. It was as if, by sending our daughter to be educated with the island children, we were casting a vote of confidence in the community, we were electing to join in rather than live our lives on the periphery of their society, with only perfunctory *Yiassus* and *Kali meras* in the shops to connect us. That was the truth of it.

One morning when I was shopping in the village, several of the mothers of children in Orla's class came up to me at different intervals in the street or in the baker's or butcher's.

"*Possos vathmos echi?*" they asked. (What level does she have?)

"I don't understand," I said. "What level of what does who have?"

"Ola," they said, (no one could pronounce the rolling 'r' in her name). "What marks did she get in the exams?"

"Exams?" I echoed blankly. They looked at me, as if I were a half-wit.

"The term exams at school, of course."

"I don't know, she didn't say anything about exams."

"Did you have exams at school, Orla?"

"Sort of, the teacher gave us some tests last week."

"And did she give you all marks?" These were six-year-old children. Exams! Marks!

"Well, she's put 9s and 10s on my copybooks. Maybe those are the marks."

154

By the next day the news had travelled round the village: the little foreigner had scored between ninety per cent and one-hundred per cent in all subjects, she who a few months ago did not speak a word of Greek.

"She must be a genius," the mothers gushed. "Because you and your husband could not have helped her."

They were right about our lack of ability to coach the child. We could not keep up with her. Now, when Elias or Maria or anyone else said something we could not understand, Orla would translate fluently. When strangers heard her speaking with a perfect Parian accent, they assumed that one of her parents must be Greek. I really had to push myself to read and write Greek better in order to help Orla with her homework and to be able to keep my side of the conversation up at the name-day parties and the other social events to which we were invited. I abandoned my textbooks for a while and learned to read and write from Orla's school reader.

Since Orla broke the ice, many other foreign children have attended the school in Parikia and in general their experience, according to their parents at any rate, seems to have been much more positive than that of our daughter. Kyria Dolkas resigned when her husband was transferred to another part of Greece and none of the other teachers seemed to be as old-fashioned or as authoritarian as she.

Chapter Eleven

New House

Early one Saturday morning towards the middle of our second year in Villa Ariadne, there was a loud banging outside our bedroom window. Looking out I saw a stranger standing on a ladder hammering a placard onto the front wall of the house. I went out to see what was going on. A large piece of wood, painted white, proclaimed in Greek and in English, *Politei. For Sale*, in giant red letters.

"What on earth is this about?" I asked the man on the ladder. "We've rented this house for a whole year from Nomikos."

"Don't ask me," replied the voice from above. "I'm only doing what I was told. Nomikos is selling the house."

We tracked our landlord down to his usual haunt, a little *ouzoria* in a cul-de-sac near his house. "Kyrie Nomikos, what does this *For Sale* sign mean on the wall of our house? You know we have paid you a year's rent in advance."

"Bah! The sign. Don't worry about that, don't worry at all." He threw his head back, lifting his chin and raising his eyes in the emphatic Greek way of saying no.

"What do you mean, don't worry? Is the house for sale or is it not?"

"Of course not."

"So why put up a *For Sale* sign?"

Nomikos downed his *raki* and called for another. He appeared to have forgotten our question, a common trick of his when he did not want to deal with a problem.

"Kyrie," I prompted him, "the sign on the wall of our house."

"Yes, yes, the sign. Well, you see, my nephew wants me to sell it. Can't wait till I die, wants to get his hands on some of my money now, the greedy pig."

"So, your nephew wants you to sell the house, and you had a *For Sale* sign put up, but you're not going to sell it."

"Never while I live. The sign will keep him happy for a while."

"And what are we going to do with the people who see the sign and call into the house wanting to buy it?"

"Just send them to me. I'll deal with them."

"And how will you deal with them?"

"I'll ask them for three million drachmas. That'll frighten them off."

"That's all very well, Kyrie Nomikos, but what if they're rich Germans or Swiss people? Three million might not be so much to them."

"Well then, I'll ask five million if they agree to three, and I'll up the price to seven if they agree to five million drachmas. Don't worry, I'm not going to sell the house. You can stay there."

Nomikos seemed determined to keep his avaricious

nephew at bay. But he was already over ninety and, hardy as he seemed, he would surely succumb before too long to either the sustained pressure of his nephew or to liver disease, the result of a lifetime of intemperate ouzo and *raki* consumption. And then we would be homeless.

That is how our decision to buy our own house came about. Greece had applied to join the European Common Market and we knew that, when that happened, the house market on Paros and elsewhere on the Greek islands would be flooded with high-earning Northern Europeans anxious to have their own place in the sun. Already there was a trickle of wealthy Germans who had bought land and houses on Paros. Rents would certainly increase, with the result that we would no longer be able to afford to live on Paros. Unless we had a place of our own.

We set about looking for somewhere to buy by asking everyone we knew – the foreigners, the shopkeepers, the bank clerks, my students, even Brylcreem in the post office – if they knew of anywhere for sale. Our idea was to buy some land with an old house or stable on it, something that could be renovated gradually over time, as money and strength allowed.

We were shown crumbling ruins, more roundy rock than upright wall, on stony hillsides, with no access except on foot along tortuous donkey-paths, with no water and no electricity anywhere near the property. All the rebuilding work, therefore, would have to be done manually as no cement mixer could get near the place. Water would have to be carried up in barrels from the nearest well (if there was a well), on the backs of donkeys. Every nail, every plank of wood, and bag of cement would have to be carried up those rocky tracks. Re-building would be a costly enterprise in terms of human sweat as well as money.

The prices the owners of these properties asked seemed to us to be extortionate. It was clear that the cheap years of living on Paros were coming to an end. The islanders could sense that a tourist wave was about to engulf the island as it had Mykonos and Rhodes and the other tourist islands years before, with the result that suddenly every metre of land was becoming as valuable as if it were in the centre of Paris and not in the countryside on Paros. I could understand the sharp rise in prices. When demand grows for land on a small island, property is at a premium, as it is in a city centre. Besides, when someone contemplates selling land or a house which may have been in the family for generations, they often do so reluctantly and the high price they demand is part of their self-justification strategy for the sale of their heritage to strangers.

"We're not rich Germans," we would protest when some farmer quoted us a price for a complete ruin with a few bushes around it which would buy a small house in good condition in the centre of Dublin. "Please don't give us those telephone figures. Give us a real price."

No deal. Manolis or Stamatis, or whoever, was not impressed by the poor mouth. They knew that if they held out, some wealthy German, Dutch or Swiss buyers would eventually turn up and pay the asking price without question. After months of searching for a place of our own, and of referring dozens of potential buyers of Villa Ariadne to Nomikos, we became dejected. It was becoming clear that we could not afford to buy even a stable on this island. We would have to leave sooner rather than later. But Paros had become very dear to us and we could not bear the thought of having to leave it.

Detach from the object of your desires and you will find peace. Desire is the enemy of happiness. This, rather crudely put tenet of Buddhist philosophy is something which I found difficult to understand when I first read it at the age of twenty. Now, over a decade later, I was about to see it work in practice. Really because we had not much choice in the matter, I stopped looking so urgently for a house on Paros. I managed to detach myself from my need to find somewhere to live and to put my desire on the back burner of my mind. That is when I discovered that when you are not looking for something desperately, when you allow other possibilities to exist, that is when you find what you want. Which is not to say that you have to give up your dream or abandon your goal before you can get your wish. No, you simply stop being so desperate, being so needy, you detach from desire and you hold your dream gently in the quiet place of the heart. You become open to considering something different. You are ready for serendipity.

It was a cold February day. The wind blew off the sea and got in between our ribs and we were chilled from the inside out. After dropping Orla off at school, I needed something warm to thaw out my frozen hands and legs which had taken the brunt of the icy north wind on the bike-ride to Parikia. The wind moaned like a banshee around the street corners in the village as I battled my way towards the heat of the pot-bellied stove in Dinosaki's. The usual suspects had gathered around the stove and an animated buzz of conversation drifted, along with puffs of smoke and steam from cups of coffee, to the high ceiling and clouded the ever-watching face of Dinosaki's priestly father. Sheila was there, chatting in her shamingly fluent Greek to one of Dinosaki's sons. Annie and Louisa were holding court at their window table. Deborah was sketching, as usual; and Stefan was recounting stories from his last fishing trip. It was too early in the day for Doctor Dick to make an appearance. Somebody made way for the frozen newcomer and I warmed myself at the stove. After a few moments, the door of the kafeneion opened again, letting in another blast of freezing air and Penelope blew in, carrying an enormous brown paper parcel. She was on her way to the post office to mail a wall hanging she had made for a customer in Frankfurt. I moved up and she squeezed another chair into the circle around the stove.

"I've met a very interesting German woman, an artist of some sort, who lives in a really remote place at the other side of the island. Somewhere between Naoussa and Marpissa. I've never been there but from what she says it's a special kind of place and very beautiful. She's invited me to visit her tomorrow, would you like to come with me?" she asked me.

The next day was my day off, so away I went on our motor-bike to meet Penelope. After Naoussa the tarred road ended and the dirt road towards Marpissa was as rutted, uneven, and full of holes as a tin roof in a shanty town. The trenched and treacherous ruts were brimming with the recent rain water, so the going was slow, wobbly, and precarious. A feeble sun kept us from being frozen to the handlebars of our motor-bikes as we rode along a broad valley, passing the dramatically Gothic mass of Naxos. The light was so sharp and clear that you felt if you reached out, you could almost touch Naxos and you could see individual houses on the hill high over the port. It was one of those magical winter days when everything you looked at had a clear definition. Almost two-dimensional, like a cardboard cut-out on a stage set. So sharp and clear and tangible that it looked unreal. The whole world was in focus and you were effortlessly part of the clarity of it all. Detached, and integrated at the same time.

After two or three miles, following Petra's instructions, we turned left off the main road onto an even narrower and more rutted track. It snaked up towards the mountain between tumbling, dry-stone walls. When we could ride no further, we left our motor-bikes under an enormous plane tree which, like most of the trees on Paros, violently signalled the direction of the prevailing winds in its tortured leaning branches. After fifty metres or so, we came to an overgrown street which poured in a torrent of polished marble rocks down the side of a hill. Abandoned houses, some with their roofs still intact and their doors locked, lined one side of the street. On the other side were the ruins of stables and barns. Two or three of the houses looked as if they had been lived in until recently or might still be inhabited in the summer. There was no child's cry, no radio music, no smell of cooking, nothing but the mysterious, seamless, quiet of a deserted human habitation. The sense of absence. The faint odour of loss.

At the top of the street, where it curved and began to rise even more steeply, we came upon what must have been the heart of the hamlet, a stone well around which were built four cement basins, used perhaps as animal drinking-troughs and for washing clothes. An inscription cast in concrete on the wall behind the well proclaimed that this well had been built by the community of Kostos for the people of Isterni.

Petra lived in the house beside the well. We found her dyeing batik headscarves to sell in the tourist shops in Naoussa. A tall, spare woman in her late twenties with shorn fair hair and distant blue eyes, Petra had something of the appearance and, I imagined, the spirit of Joan of Arc. She was living like a nun, celibate and alone. None of the foreigners on the island knew her, had even heard of her. Penelope had overheard her speaking Greek in the post office in Naoussa and that is how we came to Isterni. I wanted to know how she had come here to such a remote corner of the island and why.

Over lunch, she told us her story. She spoke slowly and carefully in the manner of someone who was suspicious of what people said, including herself, someone who distrusted verbal expression. She told us in her excellent, heavily-accented English that two years before, when she was working in Munich, she had needed to change her life. She had arrived at a crossroads and needed to find a new direction, so she had put an advertisement in a newspaper looking for a travel companion to go to Greece with her for a year. An architect called Herman had replied and they had set out on their odyssey, not knowing where they wanted to settle in Greece. Like Saint Helena they had come to the island by chance when the boat on which they were travelling to Samos was stormbound on Paros. They decided to stay where the gods had cast them up. Both wanted solitude in as remote a place as was possible on a small island. Thus they had searched until they found Isterni. Herman and she, with Teutonic thoroughness, had tracked down the absent owner of this almost derelict house and had made a deal with him: restoration of the house over two years in return for no rent. They had worked like slaves for a year. They bought a donkey and dragged wood and stones up the hillside to repair the house. They plastered and painted; they repaired the roof and the doors and window frames; they dug birds' nests out of the chimneys and got the bread-oven working again. They re-flagged the floors and pruned the vine on the terrace. They planted a protective fence of bamboos in the garden and grew their own vegetables.

"Herman and me, we did not become lovers, that was not a part of our deal," said Petra, who had become surprisingly expansive as she warmed her vocal chords. "We lived like brother and sister, but we had to tell the neighbours that we were a couple. To avoid scandal." There was something so stern and reserved about the woman that I did not dare ask how it had been possible for a young man and a young woman to live together in such a remote place, going nowhere and knowing nobody else, without succumbing to a need to find some physical comfort. I was making the assumption, of course, that both of them were heterosexual.

After the agreed year Herman had left Paros and returned to his architectural practice in Germany. Petra was not ready to go and so here she was, living like a hermit, only leaving Isterni to go into Naoussa once a month to buy supplies of coffee, matches and paraffin for the lamps and to collect mail from the post office. She bought all her food from Zacharias, a farmer who lived down the valley, about twenty minutes' walk from her house. She lived on bread, hard cheese, olives, vegetables and fruit in season and occasionally a few eggs, if Zacharias's hens were laying.

Petra spoke what sounded to me like fluent Greek. She had taught herself, she said, from children's comic books and by practising with Zacharias and his family and with Antonina.

Antonina was a real nun who lived in her own monastery on the hill opposite Isterni. Petra was now in full flight; her voice grew excited as she told us Antonina's story. A native Pariani, she had been brought by her parents to Philadelphia as a child. Her father opened a Greek restaurant there and when she was a teenager,

Antonina helped him to run it. One day while serving mousaka and a Greek salad to a customer, Antonina, whose name at that time was Kristina, heard the voice of St Anthony exhorting her to return to her native island to found a monastery there. She changed her name to Antonina and returned immediately to Paros where she found a high place from which she could see the church of St Anthony, which is on the top of a conical hill above Marpissa. There the young Antonina had built her monastery on land donated by a childless farmer. In the forty years since then she had forgotten any English she knew and rarely left her monastery.

At this point in Petra's tale, Penelope broke in. "I've known Antonina for years. How is she? I haven't seen her in ages. She's the one who taught me how to weave. She makes the most wonderful blankets and sheets on her loom. That's how she survives, by selling her weaving. And on alms, of course."

Petra looked quite put out by the announcement of Penelope's prior friendship with Antonina. Such a reclusive person might not make friends easily, I thought, so when she did she probably wanted them for herself. She continued her story, establishing the closeness of her friendship with the nun. Once a week, she told us, she walked for an hour to reach Antonina's monastery. There she would spend the day with Antonina making candles, baking bread, or washing wool for carding and spinning. They talked a lot while they worked, Petra said, and that is how she had become so fluent in Greek. Penelope was really fluent and could read and write Greek very well. Much better, I suspected than Petra. I did not want the German woman to try to compete with Penelope in the language as well as the friendship stakes, so I suggested that we might take a stroll around Isterni. Besides, I was intrigued by the place and wanted to explore it. I was fascinated by the silence that was the absence of the people who had once lived in the abandoned houses. It was not, I thought now, a melancholy silence since I had learned from Petra that most of the former inhabitants still lived nearby, down below in the valley, like Zacharias, Petra's farmer from whom she bought her food.

After a frugal lunch, we set off up the mountain along a goat-track. We climbed through banks of daisies which sprouted from every crevice in the rocks. The anemones I loved were everywhere and large purple periwinkles. The rocky torrent of a path was only suitable for fit mountain goats. Penelope and I puffed up the steep gradient, the bitter wind whipping our hair like lashes across our faces. Petra walked ahead, showing no strain, her arms swinging, her back as straight as a poker. She was a rock woman, like her name, inured to hardship and to cold.

A magnificent Van Gogh purple clump of irises flagged us down as we reached the top of the hill. I ran over to see them, and, stooping down, saw the house half-hidden behind bushes. "Oh, I didn't realise anyone was living here," I said to Petra.

"There isn't. The house is abandoned, like all the others."

Below us the valley spread out like a woven blanket: wide stripes of green fields and olive groves and narrower, grey, winding threads of paths and tracks. From up here we could see Antonina's monastery opposite and look up, up to the soaring sharp pinnacle of Mount Profitas Elias in the ink-blue distance. It was like looking out from an eagle's nest. It was perfect.

"Do you know who owns the house?" I asked Petra.

"Yes, Stelios, a farmer who lives beside Zacharias. In fact, he wants to sell it. A German came here a few months ago, he was very interested, but he didn't buy it in the end."

We beat our way through hindering thistles to the house. It was a small stone farmhouse, typical of the cube-shaped, two-roomed island houses. Built with its back into the mountain, it seemed to grow out of the rock. In front of the house was a narrow terrace of cracked flagstones in danger of slipping over the restraining terrace wall. From here you could see three threshing-circles, like fairy rings blessing the valley.

The house was roofless, its window and door frames long gone, so that its gaping openings had the appearance of the desperate, hungry mouths of nestlings whose mother had left them to eternal hunger. Inside the house hilly mounds of dried seaweed, out of which stuck broken bamboo canes and bits of yellowed plaster, reached halfway up the walls from which all the plaster had fallen. Beside the main house stood a much older-looking structure, mostly in ruins but with an enormous bread-oven still intact.

"Stelios said that this was the bakery for the village of Isterni before the war. Apparently at that time about eighty people lived here," Petra told us.

All houses have their own atmosphere, they give off vibrations, even ones as abandoned as the little farmhouse in Isterni. They can tell you whether the inhabitants are or were content with their lot in life, whether there has been serious unhappiness or conflict within the walls. They sing of joy as well as of sadness. What the ruined house in Isterni told me was that while the people who had lived there might not have been wildly happy, they were relatively content with their lives and had only left the place because they had to find work elsewhere or because they no longer wanted to live on the outskirts of a deserted village. They were frugal people who had used the natural building materials around them to build their house and later had taken what they could when they abandoned the place to re-use in the building of a new house. That is why all the doors, the door frames, the window frames and the roof beams were missing.

"You're right," Petra confirmed. "Stelios told me he had taken all the materials he could from here when he left the place twenty years ago and he used this to build his new house down in the valley."

I looked around the rest of Stelios's abandoned domain. What had at first appeared to be a jumble of rocks, strewn along the goat-track on the way up to the house, turned out to be half a dozen disintegrating stables and other outbuildings. Dry-stone walls enclosed five terraces of land which had been clawed from the rocky mountainside centimetre by centimetre, cleared of scrub and flattened to make miniature cornfields. An enormous tree marked the end of the terraced land and a thorny evergreen bush with dark-red berries draped itself like a scarf around the side of the house. This had been the meagre farm of Stelios and his ancestors.

Standing on the cracked overgrown terrace in front of the ruined house, I looked down once more over the valley and imagined the house ringing with the noise of children. I saw animals, donkeys, goats, even a cow grazing on the green terraces. I smelled freshly-baked bread and heard bees, fat with thyme, swarming in their hives. The place could be like that again. A narrow shadow fell over the nearest threshing-circle. Looking up I saw a lone kestrel hanging on a wave of air and I knew that I had found the place we had been looking for. For here was a high place where you could breathe mountain air, from where you could see the stars, where you could stretch to the mountains and to the sky and bow to the broad valley at your feet. A creative place. A minor Olympus. A place where mere mortals could live with small gods.

Petra told me the price Stelios had agreed with the German. In this isolated place Stelios had obviously not heard of the inflated sums being asked for similar ruins near Parikia. It was a fair price. I felt sure Rory would agree that Isterni was worth getting into debt for. The next day I took him proudly to show him Isterni. He came, he saw and he was conquered.

The buying of the house was a prolonged drama in which there was a cast of half a dozen. In the first act, Petra took us to meet Stelios. Nothing was said, directly, about the house for sale. We were introduced as residents of Parikia who liked Isterni very much. It is wise to move slowly when you have almost got what you want. You do not want to frighten your quarry at the last moment. Next we involved Andreas, our Parosporos neighbour and friend, to act as go-between. While I spoke reasonably good Greek, Rory had not had to make the same effort (he did not have to go to all those name-day parties) and neither of us trusted ourselves enough in the language to carry out the sort of complicated legal transactions involved in house-buying and land deals.

Andreas, Petra, Rory, myself and the children then visited Stelios and his wife, Agrioula, to play out Act Two. The scene was Stelios's small kitchen where Agrioula plied us with hunks of hard cheese and slabs of her home-made bread and Stelios filled tiny glasses with dark red wine and

170

raki and everyone, except our children, said *Yamas* and *Stin Yassas* and clinked their glasses and talked for at least half an hour about everything except the business which had brought us to Pandelis. Orla and Fiona were given small white plates of *glyka*, sticky preserved fruits. As usual, they found it too sweet and whispered to me, "Do we have to eat it, Mammy?"

And I replied, "Yes, you do. And it's rude to whisper."

Orla played her part and captivated the old couple with her recitations of poems and prayers she had learned at school. Finally, Andreas brought up the subject of the house for sale as if it were a by-the-way, unimportant item of conversation. But negotiations could not start yet. There was a short intervening act, entitled the Decline and Fall of the Highest Farmhouse in Isterni. Stelios took centre stage to tell us the history of his family farmhouse. It was not as old as the bakery, having been built at the end of the thirties with money sent to his father by a brother in Australia who had become wealthy. It replaced an older house which had stood beside the bakery. Stelios had five brothers and sisters and all of them had had their assigned roles in looking after the goats and the donkeys and the cow and helping their parents with their work. His mother ran the bakery and his father kept bees and worked on the little farm as well as doing odd building-jobs in the area. "We were happy there," the lugubrious Stelios said wistfully, "even though we had very little money and not a lot of food." After his parents died and all his brothers and sisters had left Paros, Stelios had bought land in the valley and had moved down, taking most of his building materials with him. Now he needed money to give to his son who wanted to start a tourist business in Naoussa and that is why he was selling his old home in Isterni. Stelios knew

171

that we knew how much money he had asked from the German and he did not try to increase it. So the price was settled without more ado. There remained the problem of the lack of a roof. We wanted a roof on the house as soon as possible so that we could start the renovation work. Stelios agreed to wait to close the deal until the roof was on. That way, Andreas believed, the job would be done quickly, as Stelios's builder neighbours might be more willing to oblige their relative more promptly than foreign strangers.

"You'll have to go to Zacharias to arrange for a new roof," Stelios told us. "He's a good builder. He's from Isterni, too. His family home is where Petra lives now."

Twenty minutes on foot across the fields took us to Zacharias's house. As we approached, a tall thin figure wearing a battered straw hat came springing out of his vineyard towards us. The first thing I noticed about Zacharias was the saintly expression on his face. Not an aesthete, not the stern saint of the church icons, but a kind, open-faced, smiling, even innocent-looking saint. His handshake was sincere and his eyes were welcoming. In the twenty years since we first met him, Zacharias's warm welcome has never cooled. This elderly, immensely energetic farmer/builder and his tiny, bright-eyed wife, Maria, were to become our dearest Parian friends. We go to visit them as soon as we arrive each year.

"We knew you were here," they say, "we saw your light on the hill. *Kalos elate*. Welcome back to Paros." And they embrace us as warmly as if we were their lost children.

Maria and Zacharias load us with presents from their farm, watermelons, potatoes, tomatoes, lemons, grapes, cucumbers and eggs so that we have to take rucksacks with us to carry it all back to Isterni. And Zacharias, who knows how fond we are of his rich red wine which tastes like port, fills a couple of bottles for us to take as well. Their unchanging lives, their old-fashioned hospitality and politeness, their unfailing kindness is reassuring, comforting, necessary.

The house in Isterni was roofed within a week by Zacharias and his brother Nikolas. The closure of the deal took place a few weeks later in the *plateia* in Parikia. Stelios, like many peasant farmers in Ireland, did not trust cheques or banks. He wanted all the money in cash. Rory had, in the meantime, returned to Ireland to arrange the loan and to bring the money into Greece. We changed it into drachmas, counted it out in thousand drachma notes and put it into a plastic bag in bundles.

Stelios was standing beside his donkey waiting for us under a tamarisk tree at the corner of the *plateia*. A squat, weather-beaten man with bandy legs, he stood with his straw hat pulled over his eyes like a gaucho who did not want anyone to recognise him. We handed over the money in the plastic supermarket bag as inconspicuously as we could in the middle of a busy square. Stelios took it quickly and disappeared behind some oleander bushes to count it in privacy. A few minutes later, he emerged grinning and satisfied and shook hands. Isterni was ours. We owned a ruin on the side of a mountain where thyme and oregano flourished. And so would we. And Isterni would resound again with children laughing and the smell of cooking would once more drift down the valley. I was not too sure about the goats and the donkeys. But they, too, came in time.

The last act in the drama was the paying of the tax on the property. We all had to go immediately to the tax office above the police station. Dimitris, our lawyer, the husband of another of my students, was on hand, as was our faithful translator, Andreas.

The woman in the tax office looked fierce. She told us all to sit down as if we were unruly pupils in the *demotikon*. She turned her darting black eyes on Dimitris and, without any of the usual preamble, asked him how much we had paid for the land and the house. I was astonished to hear him state an amount which was about half of what we had just handed over to Stelios in the square. The tax woman clearly did not believe the lawyer.

"And what do you say these foreigners paid you?" she asked Stelios.

He stared at the floor, hung his head like a condemned man, twisted his straw hat in his work-knarled fingers and muttered out of the side of his mouth, "Exactly what Kyrios Dimitris said, that's what they paid me."

Rory, Andreas and I then had no choice but to lie like the other two. I could not think what Dimitris was about. The true price was not that high. We had calculated the tax due and that was not unreasonable, either.

"For a house and five terraces of land on the beautiful island of Paros, you paid so little! Bah, I don't believe it," the tax woman declared, her narrowed eyes daring us to continue with the pretence.

"Let me assure you, Kyria," smoothed Dimitris, "the house is a ruin, no windows, no doors; it's been abandoned for decades. And the land is overgrown. It's a stony patch of scrubby land on a hilltop, with no olive-trees, no vines, nothing but thyme-bushes and honey-bees."

"There's no water on the land, either, they'll have to climb up and down to the well in the village for water," put in Stelios, growing courageous.

"Where is this place, Isterni? I want to go there myself

174

to see such unbelievably cheap property," Madam Tax demanded to know. Andreas explained the location of our house.

"Let's go there, right now. In your car," she commanded, looking triumphantly at Rory and myself.

"We haven't got a car," I was delighted to inform her. And I added before she proposed going in Dimitris's car, "besides, there's no road up to the house."

Reluctantly, she abandoned the idea of going to Isterni. But the game of snakes and ladders continued. "So, how do you propose to live in this inaccessible place?" Mrs Revenue demanded. "Will you fly in and out? Or maybe you intend to buy a little mule from Kyrios Stelios here."

"We'll walk up there, like Stelios and his family did for generations."

"Bah!" was her comment as she went up the snaky ladder, "You will soon tire of walking up the hill in the heat when you come out here for your summer holidays."

In the excitement of the game I found a sudden fluency in Greek and Andreas became redundant as a translator.

"Oh but, Kyria, we're not summer visitors," I told her, the dice now loaded in my favour. "We've been living here all the year round for over a year and half now. Our daughter is in the first class in the *demotikon* here in Parikia."

"I see," she conceded, looking with more interest at us, "so you know our island. You've chosen to live here." And then she rallied, "Still, I can't accept that such a paltry sum was paid for a house and land on Paros. I know what you must have paid."

She tapped her pen on the desk, pursed her lips and spat out a figure twice what we had actually paid for the place, four times the amount we had told her. Rory and I gasped.

Who could prove anything in this affair? There were no cheques, no bank drafts, just a handwritten piece of paper on which Dimitris had stated that Kyria and Kyrios Brennan had paid Kyrios Roussos the amount of drachmas he had sworn we paid. Our word against her suspicions.

"Kyria," I pleaded, becoming desperate, "as Dimitris has said, the house really is a ruin, and besides, you know that there's no water, no electricity, no road even."

"Maybe so, but land is scarce on a small island like this and you're buying five terraces of it." She sniffed and made a clicking sound with her tongue signifying disapproval.

I tossed the dice again. "True, there are five terraces. Five terraces of rocks, you couldn't grow a bush on that land. Nobody could farm it. It's worthless. In my country, Ireland, you couldn't give away such useless land."

It was a mistake. I went sliding down the snake.

The Tax Queen threw down her pen and fixed me with her glinting eyes like a hawk mesmerising a mouse before it sank its talons into it. "This is not your country. This is Greece. Here we have the sea and we have the sun. You don't have the sun in your cold, wet Ireland."

There was an icon of the Virgin and Child on the wall behind her desk and my opponent was wearing a gold cross around her neck. Inspired, I retorted, "Yes, indeed you are right, Kyria, you have the sun here in Greece. But you would agree, surely, that the sun belongs to God and cannot be taxed."

The woman looked winded, as if unfair advantage had been taken of her. She put up no further arguments. She and Dimitris bargained up and down for another ten minutes; time is plentiful in Paros. They finally agreed on exactly the sum we had, in fact, paid for the house and land in Isterni. We handed over the correct amount of tax due, everyone was satisfied and we left the office after a game of snakes and ladders which had lasted over an hour. As I closed the office door behind us I heard Madam Revenue muttering fiercely to herself, "These Irish, just like the Greeks."

At Dinosaki's a group of our friends were waiting to celebrate the buying of the ruin in Isterni. "Why did you tell her that fib?" Rory asked Dimitris.

"Can you imagine what would have happened if I'd told her the right amount in the beginning? You would have ended up paying twice the tax. As it was, she knew exactly what you had paid; she just multiplied what I told her by two. That's how we do things here. We all know the rules of the game. The important thing is to take the time to play it."

So now we had a derelict house with a roof on it, six very unstable stables and five terraces of marguerite daisies, anenomes, poppies and thyme bushes on the other side of the island, five kilometres along a dirt road from Naoussa and on the top of a hill which only a young athletic goat would find easy to climb. We had one small motor-bike to reach the place and to carry whatever wood, tools and whatever else would be needed to make the ruin semi-habitable.

The next few months were spent journeying across the island from Parosporos to Isterni carrying planks of wood dangerously strapped to the motor-bike and with assorted borrowed tools, bottles of water and packed lunches in rucksacks on our backs. Sheila's instinctively generous offer to look after the children whenever she was free from dish-washing in the taverna, left Rory and me free to work in Isterni. I used to sit on the back of the burdened Honda wearing my oldest jeans and T-shirt, holding grimly onto the planks and to my dusty husband as we bumped and rattled our way along the dirt road to Isterni. I felt like a pioneer going out to build a homestead in the Wild West, with very few resources but with a lot of optimism and energy.

When we had shovelled out the mounds of dried seaweed we discovered fairly sound polished cement floors in the two main rooms. A cheerful carpenter in Marpissa was so delighted when we asked him to make us a traditional half-door that he charged us next to nothing and also made windows in half the time it would have taken a carpenter in Naoussa. "Nobody wants the old half-doors, any more," he said. "I don't know why, they're so useful as an extra window in the summer."

Zacharias came up on his donkey and plastered the interior and exterior walls of the house and rebuilt the *pesoula*, a long, low, stone seat which runs the length of the front of many farmhouses on Paros. For most of the year the *pesoula* is where Greeks sit and eat and chat to visitors and neighbours. We would all three of us sit on the new *pesoula*, eating our lunch in the Spring sunshine, and Zacharias would decline to drink a bottle of beer with us. He could not understand foreigners' need for such gassy refreshment and preferred his flask of springwater.

When all the doors were hung and the windows installed and painted blue, when the plaster had dried and the rooms were swept clean of building debris, Rory and I whitewashed the walls and stood back dazzled by the stark, simple beauty of our emerging home.

Next we tackled the old bakery. It had three remaining walls, two were composed of the mountain at the back and the side, the third was a shared wall with the main house. The front wall had long ago collapsed into a tumble of rocks. We needed help and Zacharias was not available right away because he had to sow his crops. The *meitheal* system went into action once more. Peter Heater's brother, Paul, as strong as a Canadian bear, and newly arrived from the oilfields of Alaska, offered to help to restore the bakery. We insisted on paying him, however, as this was not going to be the work of a day or two.

A week later the bakery had four walls, a door and a window; the earthen floor had been dug down to provide standing room for six footers like Rory and everything was ready for the roof.

Rory and I learned the hard way the skilled craft of traditional roofing. First we hired Stelios's two donkeys to carry up the chestnut beams we bought from our carpenter in Marpissa. Next we carried up bundles of bamboos which Zacharias cut for us from his farm. A gang of helpers, organised by Louisa, came out to Isterni for the day all the way from Parikia to help with the arduous task of bamboo stripping. We sat on the terrace in the sun, banter and wit flashing as sharply as our knives as we stripped the bamboos.

When the beams were in place across the walls, we laid the bamboos across and tied them on. Next we placed a large sheet of polythene to act as a damp-proof membrane. The iron which would reinforce the concrete came in a big coil and had to be cut and straightened into lengths to fit the roof. Lacking a proper cutting-tool, we were forced to break the iron into the required lengths by bending it backwards and forwards until it snapped, a most tedious process. A few more simple tools would have greatly enhanced the simple life.

Finally we had to prepare the concrete for the roof. The donkeys carried up bags of sand, cement and *ammo*, which is the lime used as a mortar. We had to draw up hundreds of buckets of water from the well, pour them into barrels on the backs of the donkeys and lead the watery train up the steep track to the house.

Mixing cement is not an easy task at any time for a soft-skinned desk-worker. Mixing it with a shovel in the blistering Greek sun was a purgatory where I hope I atoned for some of my sins. Concrete is supposed to be poured, it is not meant to be dumped in uneven bucket loads, but that is all we managed to do with the lumpy mixture we produced. We had to work quickly so that the concrete would not dry out in the boiling sun before we had got it up the ladder and onto the roof. There we slung it on top of the iron bars and then tried to smooth it out as one would a cake in a baking tin. The result was a rather uneven, slightly pockmarked roof of which we were inordinately proud. Later we rather reluctantly agreed it needed to have another layer of concrete put on by professionals.

The professionals, Zacharias and his crew, did not think much of our plastic membrane. "Never heard of anyone doing that on a roof before. It won't work, it will cause condensation," they predicted. We were vindicated, however, when the next winter's rain seeped through the new roof of Helmut's house which Zacharias had put on. His bamboos ceilings were blackened and smelled of mould for a long time afterwards. Our bakery ceiling, on the other hand, has glowing golden bamboos to this day. Since then Zacharias has incorporated a plastic membrane into the roofs he makes.

When the roof of the bakery was finished and the doors and windows installed, we started the move to Isterni from Villa Ariadne. It was now summer and Orla had almost finished her first year at the *demotikon*. Even if the house had been ready before then, we could not have moved because the distance from Isterni to the school in Parikia was too great. It is about twelve kilometres and in those days there was no bus into Naoussa to catch the bus which went to Parikia. She would have to go to the small *demotikon* in Naoussa in September.

The removal process was protracted and slow. Every day we ferried what we could on the motor-bike and Sheila made trips in her old car with our mattresses and heavy luggage. Among the things she transported on the top of her car was a great, round, wooden drum, used by the electricity company for electric cables. The drum, which had been thrown into the rubbish dump, would we were sure, make a marvellous dining table some day. How we were going to get the thing up the mountain was another problem entirely, which Stelios solved by offering to lend us one of his donkeys. It is amazing the junk one collects on a Greek island. Especially when junk has a value. Apart from the fact that we could not have afforded to buy any furniture, it was not possible to buy cheap ready-made furniture on Paros. Everything was imported from Athens. We had become adept at making bookshelves from fish-boxes and at cannibalising ruined chairs, which were thrown out behind tavernas, into perfectly useful seats. All this valuable junk had to be brought over to the hills and up the mountain to Isterni.

The day came when we had emptied Villa Ariadne of all our possessions. Teddy was once again packed into Fiona's little red rucksack and we were ready to leave. Ready, but reluctant as well. We had been so happy in that little house. We would miss the tiled floors, the brown furniture, the orange-trees, the well in the garden, the

181

eucalyptus with its swing, the stone table on the terrace, the heart-lifting view over Parosporos. We would miss our dear neighbours Elias and Maria. We would miss, too, the early-morning knock on the window when Eleni, our Greek urn nymph delivered our milk and vegetables. We would miss Andreas from across the road and the Wheelers and Deborah from up the road. We would miss being able to drop into Dinosaki's every day for a drink and a gossip with Annie and Louisa or Gloria or whoever happened to be there. We would miss Emma's visits on her way to her mother-in-law with the laundry. We would even miss Doctor Dick.

By the time we had finished the litany of what we would miss, we felt quite tearful and convinced that we were moving to the deserts of outer Mongolia, instead of to a wonderful house with a wonderful view. We would find wonderful neighbours in Isterni too, we told ourselves. And after all, Paros is a small island. It was possible to travel its furthest distance, even in those days, in less than an hour, even on a slow motor-bike on bad roads. We could still see our old friends from the Parikia end of the island. We could still drop into Dinosaki's once every few weeks or so and find out where the next party was being held.

Into the inventory of losses and gains I added the fact that I would no longer be able to continue my English classes, because the distance was just too great and the roads too poor to travel on a regular basis. No doubt I would find new students in Naoussa and learn about their love lives.

When I went to tell Nomikos that we were moving, his eyes filled with tears although he had known, of course, that we had bought a house in Isterni and we had given him months of notice. He held me to him and his shoulders shook. I was surprised. I had not known that he was that fond of us. Then his small hand crept up towards my breasts and he took one and squeezed it gently. "Just like my Flora's breasts," he said and cried all over again. Flora was his wife who had died thirty years before.

Elias, Maria and Eleni made us promise to come to visit them as often as we could. Our last party at Villa Ariadne seemed to last for days and to have been attended by hundreds of people who drank barrels of wine. Everyone said they would come over to see us in Isterni when we had had a chance to settle in. At last Orla and Fiona and I packed ourselves into Sheila's car with the last bits of baggage and Rory followed us to Isterni on the motor-bike.

Chapter Twelve

New Neighbours

The new community into which we moved was a scattered agricultural one in which many people were related by blood or marriage and, of course, everyone knew everyone else. It was important, therefore, to be regarded as a *kalo pedi*, a good kid, if one was to live harmoniously among them. Working side by side with Zacharias and Nikolas, we got to know the family histories of many of our neighbours. Neighbours is probably not too close a description because, apart from Petra's, only four other houses on the hill of Isterni were still occupied. Everyone else lived down in the valley.

Spiros, his wife Eleni and their adult son Pandelis lived below us to the right. Spiros had sold their old home to Helmut, a German who came to Isterni several times a year. The two men drove their bleating, bell-ringing goats past the bottom of our land every day on their way to the well. If we were on the terrace we would wave and shout

Kali mera and they would wave back. After a while, they took to coming up to visit us, often bringing presents of fruit or vegetables. Spiros was in his seventies, a mountain goat of a man, with a bulging bad eye and arthritic hands grotesquely twisted like olive-roots. Pandelis was the youngest of his three sons and the only one unmarried and still living on the farm. The others had left the island to work as builders' labourers in Athens.

Sometimes we felt that our new neighbours firmly believed that foreigners, especially foreigners who were not manual workers, were incapable of doing anything practical. We were always being told that things would not work, that this was not the way to do whatever it was.

"*Tha pes kato*" (that will fall down) was Pandelis's favourite remark to us. The first time he said it was when he came up one day as we were building an *avli* or pergola. The front of the house in Isterni faces south-west, a wonderful orientation in sun-starved Ireland, but a very hot place to be in the summer after eleven in the morning on Paros. The thick stone walls of the house absorb the full furnace-blast of the sun and act like storage heaters, blasting heat into the rooms at night. We needed to provide shade so that we could sit and eat at the *pesoula* without risking sunstroke and we also had to find some way of cutting down on the amount of heat which penetrated the walls. The answer was to build an *avli* along the front of the house. The traditional method of *avli* construction is to build stout, stone columns at a distance of a few metres from the front wall of the house, to insert wooden beams at intervals into the walls and to rest the end beams on the stone pillars. Vines are grown over the *avli* to provide shade or, more often today, a cement roof is built on the beams, creating an open-sided room. The *avli* is where Greek

186

families live in summer, only entering the house to cook and to sleep.

Thick stone pillars would have blocked or interrupted our magnificent view over the valley below and the mountains beyond, so we compromised by erecting wooden poles on which we constructed the *avli*. We decided against planting a vine to provide shade because the terrace was so exposed to the prevailing winds that we did not think it would grow. So we tied bamboos onto the overhead beams, thereby achieving instant slatted shade. According to Pandelis the whole lot would fall down and be blown away by the first real winds of the winter. However, like the ceiling of the bakery, the *avli* is still fairly sound twenty years later, much to Pandelis's headshaking wonderment. Over the years, Spiros and Pandelis, their straw hats shading their expressions, would sit for ages on the *pesoula* examining our latest folly, shaking their heads and clicking their tongues, telling us what would fall down next. Rory and I did not bother arguing; we just poured them another glass of ouzo, handed round a plate of olives and asked questions about Isterni in the old days.

Pandelis, whose name means "all delights" in Greek, was a mournful soul who always had a pain in some part of his anatomy. He believed that if he could get the right medicine from Germany all would be well. There was no good medicine in Greece, according to him. Helmut was requested to bring a plethora of medication each time he came. Pandelis was probably in his late thirties when we first met him but he seemed much older. He had the air of a man who had never been a boy, who had not had the luxury of either a spent or a misspent youth, who had never, in fact, been young. He wore his father's cast-off clothes, which were a good deal too small and tight for his powerful frame. His tattered trousers were at half-mast and his long brown arms hung awkwardly from his father's short shirt sleeves. A deeply religious man, he was a follower of the rites of the old calender. According to this, Easter and the other orthodox feast-days are celebrated according to the Julian calender and not according to the Gregorian calender, used by the modern Greek church. Antonina was another old-calender follower and Pandelis attended services in her monastery, celebrating Easter on different days to his elderly parents.

Spiros told us about the origin of Isterni. Originally people from the village of Kostos, which we could see on a hill on the other side of the valley, had come over to Isterni to graze their animals in the summer. Some of them built temporary summer-houses in Isterni to save themselves the long trek back to Kostos every night. Gradually these families remained in Isterni the whole year round and built proper houses and stables. Before the Second World War there had been around ten families in the hamlet, each with six or seven people. They had been a largely self-sufficient little community with the common family name of Roussos. Zacharias's father had supplied the coffee and sugar they needed in his tiny grocery shop by the well and our house, as we knew, had been the bakery.

During the war Paros had been occupied, like many Greek islands, by both the Italians and the Germans. It was interesting to hear different opinions of the occupiers from different neighbours. Some of them considered the Italians to have been the worse, because they had pilfered chickens and goats, while the Germans had apparently paid for the food they requisitioned. The valley below Isterni had been turned into an airstrip and planes had taken off from here to attack Crete. People starved during the war, Spiros told us with a sad shake of his head, especially in Parikia and Naoussa.

During the impoverished post-war period, as in so many villages throughout Greece, an exodus took place from Isterni, a haemorrhaging of young people to find work in Athens and other Greek cities. The older farmers like Zacharias, Spiros and Stelios, the former owner of our house, also left the hamlet, building new houses in the valley nearer their fields and vineyards. Within five years Isterni had become an almost deserted village.

When we arrived there in 1978, all but Petra's house along the single street were abandoned. But further up on the hill, four houses were still occupied. Helmut came from Germany to Spiros's old house in spring and autumn. Nikolas, the brother of Zacharias, lived with his wife and family on the headland beyond Helmut. An old couple, Kyria Anna and her husband Costas, were Helmut's near neighbours. Manolis and his three children lived in a ramshackle house beside Nikolas.

Here was a most unusual situation, a Greek man looking after young children on his own. He was not a widower; his wife had run off some years before, rumour had it, with another man, leaving Manolis with a daughter, Agrioula, and two small boys, one of whom was mentally retarded. The children ran wild. Evangelis, the retarded child, took everything he fancied and was to become something of a menace to us over the years. Poor Manolis did his best, but he was an epileptic and not, as we say at home, the "full shilling" himself.

At the age of fifteen Agrioula ran off with a man twenty years older than her who came to buy goats from her father one day. She now lives with him and her large brood of children on a remote mountain farm on the high slopes of

Mount Profitas Elias. Manolis struggled on, trying to keep his farm and his family together. One evening just as we were setting off to have dinner with Spiros and Eleni, Manolis appeared at our house. He was driving his herd of goats over the mountain. He seemed unwell, so we gave him a glass of water and asked him to sit down for a while. Before he could sit, he was thrown to the ground by a severe epileptic fit. I had never seen one before and was terrified that Manolis had had a heart attack and might die. Rory knew what to do, thankfully, and when the poor man had recovered somewhat, we helped him back to his own house. "What would happen if Manolis had a fit near a well?" Rory wondered prophetically.

Two years afterwards, one frosty winter morning, that is exactly what happened. Manolis did not die in the well, they managed to fish him out alive. He was put on a tractor and brought to Naoussa where the doctor could do nothing for him and said he needed emergency treatment in the hospital in Syros. It angered us to learn later that if Manolis had had money, they could have got a helicopter to take him immediately to Syros. As it was, the poor man was bundled onto a caique to make the two-hour journey in a Force 6 wind. He died before the boat reached Syros, his lungs punctured by his broken ribs.

Antonina, who was a relative of Manolis's deserting wife, took in the two boys to bring them up in the monastery. Evangelis, however, seems to haunt Isterni. On still evenings his loud and melodious voice can often be heard, from high in the branches of the eucalyptus tree outside his old home, singing a zany mixture of radio ads for soap powder mingled with verses of *Kyrie Eleision* and other church hymns.

That first summer we spent in Isterni, Kyria Anna and

her shadowy husband, Costas, still lived in a house we called the *castro*, because it was built like a small fortification on the hill. The old couple had reared six children in the two-roomed house which grew organically out of the rocks. It was like a cave sculpted by the wind, with breathtaking views over the sea and the island of Naxos. All six children had gone off to work and marry in Athens and the old couple were alone and lonely. If we happened to pass the *castro* near any meal-time, we were invariably brought in to share their wonderfully nutritious and simple meal. Everything on the table had been produced by themselves: the chicken, the sea salt, the bread, the cheese, olives and olive-oil, potatoes, vegetables and fruit. The only thing bought in a shop was the coffee and the paraffin for the lamps. Kyria Anna, a large robust lady with a wonderfully humorous face, did all the talking, her husband was a Jack Sprat of leanness who kept his head on one side and his opinions to himself.

Costas died the following year, leaving Kyria Anna alone on the mountain with her goats and chickens. Despite the persistent disapproval of her children, she insisted on staying on in Isterni by herself. Several times I met her clopping down the hill on her donkey, seated side-saddle, heels gently kicking its flanks, on her way to the few terraces of land she owned near Lefkes, at least twelve kilometres from Isterni. She was going to look after her ancient olive-trees.

"Why should I leave this place where I have spent more than half a century?" she would shout as she passed me. "What would I do without my animals in those boxy apartments in Athens? How could I breathe that air?"

"You're right, Kyria Anna, Isterni is where you belong," I would shout back. And I would stand to watch her plump black figure, wedged between reed baskets on the donkey, bobbing down the path until she became a small question mark in the valley. Her children and their children used to come for holidays to the ugly garage-shaped house which one of her sons had built on the track leading to Isterni. The house, where they were reared, was "too small" for the city dwellers to spend holidays. Her children went on and on to us about their stubborn, foolhardy mother.

"She'll break her leg, running after those goats on the mountain. And then what will she do? It's not right for a woman of her age to live alone like that."

Poor Kyria Anna did not fall running after goats. She fell victim to a bad dose of bronchitis and had to be brought to hospital in Athens. There her son must have finally worn her down. Her wonderful house in Isterni was put up for sale. Battista spent a hectic month whacking donkeys and mules up the hill with cement and sand to "restore the house" in order to sell it for a high price. The rounded walls which followed the curve of the rocks and the contours of the hill were straightened out, right-angled into line. The cavernous stables below the house were regimented into squareness by cement blocks and their mouths covered with blank doors. The *castro* became another blockhouse and was sold, for a high price, to a foreigner who rarely visits the place.

We saw Kyria Anna a few more times before she died. She would come to visit Isterni, slumped, a defeated woman, in the back of her son's car. She looked slighter, reduced, all her mountain vigour drained away by the polluted Athens air and the noisy cramped apartment she lived in with her son's family. She would look wistfully at the hill but was unable to climb up to her old house. I am sure her family intended to be kind and that they acted out of concern for their old mother. Sometimes, however, people only become really old and infirm when their choices are cut off and they are treated by their family like children, unable to make their own decisions.

We had a heated discussion once with Petros, a Greek architect friend of ours. We were bemoaning the destruction, as we saw it, of Kyria Anna's house. "The old ways of building, using local materials, rock, wood, bamboo, fitting the houses into the landscape, so that they seem to grow there, that's best," we argued. "The proportions are right, there's a human scale about those buildings, the golden mean and all that. These modern, cement-block monstrosities, bristling with steel rods which poke through the roof, these are abominations. This isn't traditional Greek architecture. It shouldn't be allowed."

"You may not like it, I certainly don't like it, but this is modern Greek domestic architecture," was his reply. "It has become the tradition. Nobody can dictate that the golden mean should be used or that traditional materials only should be used. People like these uncomplicated houses, they're cheap to build and easy to run. Those old houses, as you know yourselves, had no running water, no toilets, no showers, very little light inside, very little space indeed. Sure they look nice, sure they fit into the landscape, but the fact is that many Greeks just don't want to live in them any more, they aren't modern, they're certainly not convenient. And before you protest that mod cons can be installed in an old house and the house made more comfortable, let me say that you know as well as I do that such refurbishment often costs much more than building a brand new house."

Of course, we did not have to go to Greece to know that he was speaking the truth. At home in Ireland, too, we have criticised the fact that most of the old, traditional thatched or slated cottages have been replaced by cement-block houses with enormous picture windows and hacienda-style arches. The decreasing number of old houses that remain are often owned, as in Greece, by foreigners who decry the "destruction of the countryside" by bungalow-bliss architecture.

We needed to do something to make our own old house in Isterni more convenient to live in. It was a long, hot haul down to the well, longer and hotter carrying buckets of water up the steep, rocky track back to the house. We had to have a water supply near the house. A water diviner failed to locate any spring on the land, so we asked Zacharias to build us a cistern, before the winter rains, under the terrace in front of the house.

When the cistern was finished, Zacharias assured us it would fill to the top with water running off the roof from the winter rains. We should have enough to last for most of the year if we did not waste litres of it in a flush toilet.

For the next fifteen summers we lived without a flush toilet and showered using buckets of water drawn from the cistern. Living on an island where it often does not rain for eight months makes one very conscious of what a precious commodity water is. Not a drop is wasted; the washing-up and shower water is recycled to water the plants and if you have a flush toilet you use it very sparingly indeed.

So there we were during that first summer on the mountain – the residents of Isterni and environs: Zacharias and Maria, Manolis and his wayward children, Spiros, Eleni and the morose Pandelis, Kyria Anna, her husband Costas, and her goats, Nikolas and his family, Helmut, when he came from Munich to sunbathe on his terrace, Kyria Anna's son, Battista, and his wife and children for the month of August, and Petra making do and making batik scarves. And across the valley, on the mountainside opposite, the solitary nun Antonina, deep in candle wax, wefts and warps, ringing out her bell for prayers at dawn and dusk, a call only the pained Pandelis answered on his knees.

Nikolas, the younger brother of Zacharias, his wife Foto, their eldest son and heir Yannis, and their one remaining daughter, Constantina, farmed, by island standards, a large and prosperous farm beside Manolis. Nikolas resembled Zacharias in looks and in certain of his mannerisms and he was also kind and hospitable, but we never developed with him the kind of empathy we had with his elder brother. Constantina, a well-built girl of fifteen, with a thick mane of black hair in a plait down her back and wide guileless eyes reminded me of Cinderella, left at home to do all the dirty work from which her four sisters had escaped to Athens.

But Constantina was a cheerful girl and did not seem at all resentful. She sang to herself all day in an outhouse, well out of her mother's way, sifting the corn for grit. Sometimes I used to wander over to Nikolas's farm for a walk or to buy eggs from Foto in the cool of the evening and I would seek out Constantina and chat to her while she fed the chickens or sifted corn. Being with her was like sitting beside a slow-moving stream: one was aware that life was gently passing by underwater without ruffling the surface.

We would often see her washing the family's clothes at the village well beside Petra's house. Watching her standing there, her arms up to the elbows in soapy water, an age-old image of woman at work, I thought of the contrasting lives of girls of her age in Dublin: the cinemas, the discos, the giddy school-friends, the flirtations with boys of their own age. Constantina had left school at the age of twelve at the end of primary level. She could read and write, but had nothing to read and little occasion to write. There were no books in the house and no newspapers were ever bought. She had never been to Athens, rarely even to Parikia. She had never seen a television programme, had never been to a cinema or disco, did not know what a ghetto-blaster or a hit album were. The highlight of her life was the annual summer visits of her married sisters, bringing her new clothes and news of another world. She seemed destined to become the robust stay of the family.

But destiny can be foiled. On a yellow spring day Constantina, herding goats along a track in Isterni, met a lithe young man from Crete come to look for his grandmother's ancestral home. Constantina led him to the ruin where he took photographs for his parents in Chania. He took photos, too, of the pretty goatherd who smiled like a child into the sun. They talked for ten enchanted minutes. Next day he returned to the rock from where Constantina supervised the hobbled goats. They fell in love, were married within three months and Constantina went off to live in Crete.

Chapter Thirteen

Swallows

It was almost the end of the summer and of our second year on Paros. On a magnificent light-filled afternoon I collected Orla from a children's party. She seemed her usual dreamy self as she trailed out of the house, the white collar on her red dress slightly awry. "Mammy," she said, climbing onto the pillion seat of my motor-bike, "you know what? I want to live somewhere where they speak my language."

The child spoke fluent Greek. "Where they speak my language?" My heart flipped and I turned to look into my child's face. Was there something I had missed these past months? Had I been so involved in restoring the house in Isterni that I had not noticed some sadness in my daughter? Since those dreadful early weeks in school when she had cried every morning because she did not know which seat to sit in and had played alone in the playground with her little red car, she seemed to have settled in and to be more

197

content. Before the summer break, when we had sneaked around the side of the building to catch a glimpse of her at playtime, she appeared to be happily playing with her friend, little blonde Theoktisti from Agia Irini. The headmaster had taken her under his kind wing and she had got over her terror of Kyria Dolkas.

In fact, by the end of her first year in school, she had become something of a teacher's pet. This came about when one day we were visiting Antonina in her monastery. It was, as it turned out, a feast-day in the old calender and the small church in the monastery courtyard glowed golden in the light of Antonina's home-made, beeswax candles. Kyria Dolkas came into the church as we were lighting candles in front of an icon of the Virgin. Thinking that we had come to the monastery to celebrate the feast-day, she was most impressed and greeted us very warmly, like new converts. After that Orla had become one of her class favourites, entrusted to go to the headmaster with messages and to ring the bell when break was over. It was a pity that she would have to go to a new school in Naoussa after the holidays, but we felt that, as she survived Kyria Dolkas, and could now speak Greek fluently, our daughter should have little difficulty settling into a new school.

"I'd like to live where they speak my language." The child's face was calm and thoughtful beyond her years. She did not look unhappy; there had been no trace of sadness or anger in her voice. She had spoken matter-of-factly. For a few moments I was at a loss as to what to do, what to say. Then, as casually as I could, and half-knowing the reply my daughter would give me, I asked, "Darling, you understand Greek very well. What do you mean by 'where they speak my language'?"

"I mean where the people are the same as me, the same as you and Daddy and Fifi. The same as my grannies."

"Do you not like the people here in Greece, the children in your class?"

"Mammy, I do like the people. I didn't say I didn't like them. But they're not the same. That's all. I don't understand sometimes why they do some things. It's not like at home in Dublin."

When I told Rory about Orla's remark, he did not look at all surprised. "The child obviously wants to be somewhere more familiar, where she knows the games and the rules, where she feels that she belongs. Children are great adapters, but they also know instinctively where they fit in and where they don't." He then went on to tell me that he had been thinking quite a lot in the previous weeks about our future on Paros. I confessed that I, too, had been wondering if and for how much longer we should stay on the island.

Our lives were idyllic; we lived in our own house in a beautiful place, in a good climate; we had lots of time to spend with each other and with the children; we were able to do the writing and studying we had come to do; our friends and family loved coming to visit us. Indeed in the unpressurised atmosphere of the island we enjoyed their company more thoroughly than was possible in the bustle of Dublin.

On the other hand, our two daughters were growing. Fiona would be starting the *nipion*, the kindergarten, at the end of the summer and both of them had twelve to fourteen years of schooling to go through. Should we stay on the island and send them to primary and secondary school here? Our experience of Orla's time in the *demotikon* in Parikia was not very encouraging. Besides,

199

with a Greek education, could they get into university in Ireland? Would they thank us for keeping them out of their own country until they could make up their own minds about where they wanted to live? And now Orla had told us she did not feel she belonged here. And, besides all that, we had to ask ourselves for how much longer we wanted to live close to the breadline, without earning salaries and without the challenges of the workplace. Would we be content to continue in this idyllic Lotus-eaters' existence indefinitely?

We looked around us at the foreigners who had been living on Paros for longer than us. People like Bert and Christine had the school to keep them busy and to provide a modest income. Deborah used the island as the inspiration for her paintings and spent a quarter of each year in the United States where she sold her canvasses and earned enough to live on Paros for the rest of the year. The Wheelers had plenty to occupy them also: Clive sold his sculptures in galleries around Europe and Phoebe did all the secretarial and promotional work needed as well as looking after her family and making jam, wine and wreaths of dried flowers for sale in England. Louisa and Annie had retired and were entitled to be Lotus-eaters for as long as they wanted to. Penelope and Jean-Pierre were natural recluses, who would always work for themselves and for whom the isolation of their house on the island was a necessary protection from the outside world. Sheila seemed to have found her niche on Paros. She lived among the Greek community more than any of us. She read Greek newspapers and listened to the news on Greek radio stations. She had started an English school and was making a reasonable living. Many of the others would, we were sure, move on before too long as their money ran out or the need to live a more challenging life re-surfaced.

And then there were the grandmothers. They would not live forever. When they came to Paros to visit us, Orla and Fiona were so delighted to see them and so upset for weeks after they left. If we stayed on the island, that wonderful contact between generations would be restricted to a few weeks a year. Rory and I, who remembered being spoiled by our own grandparents, felt badly that our daughters were being deprived of the irreplaceable contact with their grandmothers. Especially as they had three grandmothers who loved children. And there is not an infinite time-frame for such relationships. Would it be fair to either our parents or our children if, by living on Paros, we were to continue to separate them for most of the year? Especially as this was not a forced separation, due to having to find work abroad, but one caused by our need to get out of the mainstream and to float quietly in gentler pools for a while.

During our first year on the island, I was convinced that our life on Paros was "the real life", that what we had left behind in busy Dublin was a half-life, a rat-race with no winners. After we had been living most pleasantly for more than a year as Lotus-eaters, albeit not in the least indolent, treacherous little doubts began to nibble like escaped white mice at the corners of the wonderful picture we had painted for ourselves. A small island is, after all, somewhat restrictive; one could quite easily be in danger of becoming a large fish in a small pond, one could perhaps fool oneself about the quality or importance of one's work; there was not enough competition, there were no really hard edges. Growing suspicious of the smooth, we began to feel a need for the rough.

After much deliberation, of making lists of the pros and cons of leaving, we came to the conclusion that life on Paros was no more "real life" than life in Dublin had been "half-life". But I also realised that, while I needed more challenges than were possible on Paros, I also wanted to live a less hectic existence than we had previously had in Dublin. Perhaps "real life" was a combination? Would the solution be to spend half the year on Paros and the other half in Ireland?

Within a few weeks, our questioning and wondering had hardened into a decision to leave Paros for part of every year and to return to Ireland to live as simply, meaning as cheaply, as we could. We would spend seven or eight months of the year in Ireland, probably in the countryside, and return to our home on Paros for the remaining four or five months. Such a division of time would mean, of course, that we could not take up normal teaching or other regular jobs, that we would have to become freelance workers and that we would really have to live frugally, without a car and other bill-generating modern conveniences, in order to save enough for the annual sojourn on Paros. The prospect of living in a beautiful place in the Irish countryside, even if the untaxable sun did not shine as much or as warmly as on Paros, excited us. Our children were delighted by the thought of seeing their grannies very often. The grandmothers were thrilled that we were bringing their beloved granddaughters back to them and relieved that we seemed to have got over our wanderlust and might settle down properly at last.

We packed our rucksacks, locked up the house in Isterni for the winter, said goodbye to our new neighbours and our old friends and returned to Ireland, happy that we would be returning after the winter. Our plans for a simple life back home did not work out quite as we had imagined, but that is a long and complicated story, for another day perhaps. In brief, we did not live in the countryside, but ended up, after many adventures in rural Ireland, back in our old house in Dublin. Our children went to the school around the corner, the one which Orla had attended two years previously. On her first day at school four-year old Fiona came home bursting with the news that, "There's another Greek girl in my class." Zara, whose father is Athenian, became a lifelong friend and visited us on Paros several times with her parents. It took Orla a few months to stop writing her name in Greek and to substitute the Latin s for the Greek *sigma*.

The three grateful grandmothers lavished affection on the delighted children and all four were the best of friends, playing cards together, way past the children's bedtime, late into the night during the holidays and eating as many sweets as they liked, away from the strict, sweet-restricting eye of mother. Rory's mother taught them how to play poker and to make fudge and his aunt instructed them in the art of bridge. My mother remembered all the poems and stories, the Irish myths and legends, she had stored up during her years as a teacher and told them again and again to her enthralled grandchildren. Watching the grey and the blonde heads bent in excited concentration over a game of cards or seeing the children walking so slowly beside their grandmothers, listening to stories of their childhoods at the beginning of the century, I knew that we had made the right decision. Within ten years all the grannies had died and we thanked the gods that we had brought the girls back to them for that precious time together.

Rory and I changed careers. He became a radio broadcaster and arts administrator and I worked for a time in a college of art as a lecturer in art history, before becoming involved in an absorbing job with a development aid agency. We tried, not very successfully perhaps, to keep our lives stress-free and unbusy. It is not very easy to live the simple unhurried life in a city where you have to travel for miles to get to work, where the social life is inviting, where you get involved in politics and campaigns of all sorts to "make the world a better place for your children and their children's children". Before you know where you are, you are right back there in the whirl and middle of things. You decide you need to go back to university before your brain rusts away completely. You do that, as well as a full-time job and looking after two very active and inquisitive children who have to be taken to ballet and Irish dancing classes, to piano and recorder lessons, to Girl Guide camps and to birthday parties all over the city. You get busier than you ever imagined you could be. And sometimes you became nostalgic for the days of the Lotus-eaters on Paros.

Like homing swallows we return to Paros faithfully every summer, but never for as long as we had intended. Life has a habit of not working out as neatly as one planned it. However, most summers Rory manages to spend three months on the island, while I, because of my job, only have a month. When people who do not know us very well ask, "Where are you going to on holidays this year?" we say "Greece."

And they say, "But didn't you go to Greece last year as well?"

And we reply, "Yes, we did, we go every year."

204

And relentlessly they press on. "How long do you go for?"

And we mumble, as if we were being forced to admit something disgraceful, "For a month or two."

And the little green god flickers in some eyes, "For a couple of months! How can you afford such a long holiday?"

And we mutter something to the effect that it's not really like a holiday, it's more like going home because we used to live there.

Then the light dawns and they pounce, "Oh, so you have a house there?"

And we mutter something about a little farmhouse, a ruin that we restored with our own hands. And they are still jealous and cannot understand how anyone can have a few months' holiday on a Greek island every summer without being very rich indeed.

Of course we are very rich. Paros is not only a holiday place for us, it is a renewing place to work, a place where we recharge our creative batteries, where we know the phases of the moon, where we can see Orion's belt and the Starry Plough every night in the clear, dark skies over Isterni, where the pace of life slows to the clop-clop of a donkey and to an evening's slow conversation on the *pesoula* with Zacharias and Maria or Spiros and Eleni. The atmosphere and landscape which inspired Rory's first prize-winning book of poetry continue to inspire him, and he has since published two more collections of poems, many of them rooted in Parian soil. For my part, I have been scribbling away in my blue Greek student's copy books: short stories, journals and what I grandly call, "random jottings of a poetic nature". I have also taken up painting and have spent many absorbed hours sketching from our terrace in Isterni or painting in my friend Alice's studio in Naoussa.

Orla and Fiona continued to come on holidays with us for many years until they were teenagers. Later on they found work in the bars and nightclubs in Parikia and rented rooms there from which they could come and go easily to the discotheques and beaches. Our little mountain eyrie in Isterni, miles from anywhere, is too remote and quiet for very sociable young women. They will come back to Isterni one day when they have had enough of life in the fast lane. Indeed last summer, Orla, tired after the year's work in London, spent two weeks in Isterni with her boyfriend and was glad of the quiet. She had not been able to go to the island for a couple of years and missed the place so much that she just had to get back there. She has forgotten how to read and write in Greek, but after a few days on Paros she can speak as fluently as ever she did in that sombre bare classroom in Parikia. Fiona has only missed one summer when she was rehearsing and acting in a play in the Edinburgh Festival.

There have been some sad changes since we left Paros in 1979. In 1980 Bert Smith, our dear friend from the Aegean School of Fine Art, died, tragically early, at the age of 40. The red wine, which he liked so much was not kind to his liver. It is only when someone is not here any more that their true worth lights up in the darkness of their absence. Especially larger-than-life people like Bert. Although Bert's laugh no longer fills his house and drives the kestrel in a flurry of wings around the ceiling and no sounds of a happy saxophone float on the evening street outside the art school, Bert lives on in the spirit of the place. Hardly a week goes by when somebody does not recall a Bert Smith story and smile at the memory. Bert's partner, Christine, stayed on Paros for a while to sort out their affairs, to sell the house, to find another director for the art school. Then she went back home to live in Philadelphia with Bert's mother, a wild and witty poet.

When I turn to remembering the past twenty years on Paros, those who no are longer present rise to the surface of my mind like phosphorus gleaming on the sea. And I am not sad, just grateful that for a time I shared the island with them. Grace is one of the luminous ones whose memory lights the street where she lived. She died suddenly in 1994. I go out of my way to walk past her neat little house in the backstreets of Parikia so that I can remember her kindness and laughter, the map of the world which took up one whole wall of her minute living-room, marked in green with places she had been and in red with the countries she planned to visit next. I remember, too, the wonderfully civilised dinner parties she gave, using her best monogrammed china, silver cutlery and starched, white linen tablecloth and napkins.

Diving was how Stefan (Count Dracula) lost his short life. On Christmas Eve 1979, the anchor of one of the ferry boats became entangled as the ship tried to leave the harbour. All efforts to release it failed. A diver was needed to go down to find and release the anchor and a reward of ten thousand drachmas was offered. Stefan, always the daredevil, took the challenge and dived down into the freezing waters of the harbour without the benefit of a wet suit or an oxygen tank. When he had not surfaced after some minutes the alarm was raised. Whether it was hypothermia or a heart attack brought on by water pressure, we never learned. Stefan was just twenty-five years old when he was buried in the cemetery in Parikia. His wife, Claudia, was left to face an unbearable Christmas and to look after their infant daughter, Miranda. They still live on Paros in a beautiful house looking out over the island of Antiparos in whose bays Stefan used to go spearfishing for octopus.

When I think of Bert, Grace and Stefan I remember true islanders, people who seemed to live most fully in small communities and who, just by being themselves, enlivened and enriched our lives and the island. In some essential way, they belonged on Paros and to Paros. If they had they lived on Bali or the Aran Islands, they would probably have fitted in there, too.

Many other people who lived on Paros for years somehow do not belong to the island. They live there as in a cocoon, with little connection with the bloodstream, the sinew and the bone of Paros. Whatever is their essence does not mingle with the essence of the island. Belonging on Paros has to do with communication which is beyond language, it has to do with giving, with respect for the Greek island way of life, without necessarily trying to become "one of the people". We foreigners will always be outsiders on Paros, as indeed are the Greeks who come from Athens to run tourist shops and restaurants in the summer. We cannot completely be part of a community where generations have lived and intermarried, where we do not have our roots, but we can still belong to Paros as her adopted children. It seems to me that islomanes are a special breed, at the same time self-sufficient and community-minded. No man, or woman, can be an island on an island, unless they are either hermits or misanthropists.

In the eighteen years since we stopped living full-time

on Paros, there have been noticeable changes in the lives of almost everyone on the island. These days hardly any foreigners live in run-down farmhouses without electricity or running water. Nowadays most of the foreign community seem to be older and richer. They live in grand, architect-designed villas, they drive cars and use mobile phones, a few of them even have swimming-pools. Many are the same people who lived on Paros in the late 1970s when we first came, so they are indeed older. They have become wealthier in different ways: a few came into inheritances, others left the island for a number of years and made a lot of money, more became part-time residents and spend most of the year earning high salaries abroad.

And, of course, many more foreigners have discovered "our" island and have come to live here. On the hill of Isterni new houses have been built, I am glad to say, in a fairly traditional style. And now we have the welcome company of wonderful new neighbours from Germany and from Athens. The abandoned village houses were bought and developed some years ago by Costas, an architect with a real feel for the place. He created half a dozen houses which were later sold to an enlightened Swiss businessman. Now we have a yoga centre in Isterni to which people come from all over Europe.

When we arrived on Paros there were very few foreigners married to Greeks. The only one I knew was our friend, Emily, from the beautiful house beside the beach at Parosporos who had married Mikalis the carpenter. Later on Sheila married a native Pariano. With the wave of mass tourism, many more foreign women have met and married island men. So that nowadays Orla's school has quite a few bi-lingual children.

As for the old-time foreign residents, our lives are more self-contained now, we do not need each others' help as before. The *meitheal* we used in the early days is defunct. We can afford to pay Albanian refugees to do the hard work. Nowadays the subject of conversation on the verandas over gin and tonic is too often of gardeners, cleaners, pool filters or solar-heating systems. Prosperity has brought creature comforts, independence, and perhaps a certain sense of splendid isolation. While it is, no doubt, much easier to throw the laundry into a washing-machine than it is to carry it to a well and wash it in cold water, or to watch an Albanian repair a leaky roof than climb up there oneself with sticky black tar, something that I valued in the old way of life has been lost.

Quite a few of our old friends have left Paros for good and each summer I miss their presence. Penelope and Jean-Pierre, Peter Heater, Louisa and Annie and Petra, the recluse of Isterni, have all gone to other lives. But some losses open doors to new friends. A year after Petra left Isterni, a young Greek family from Athens bought the house by the well. Costas and Stella and their children Giorgos and Johanna have become our good friends and an essential part of our summers in Isterni. We were glad that another house in the village became alive with children and we look forward each year to seeing them all again and to the evenings we spend on their terrace discussing the present state of Greece and the events of the past winter.

In the 1980s the tourist wave which was just beginning at the end of the 1970s changed Paros beyond recognition. An airstrip was built, more and bigger ferries came more frequently. Hotels and holiday apartments were built everywhere. With the entry of Greece into the EC and the availibility of funds, new roads were built and old roads were tarred. Good roads invite cars, tour buses, taxis, and hired motor-bikes. The noise and pollution levels rose and the whole pace of life quickened.

The villages of Parikia and Naoussa tripled in size. Lounger chairs and sun-umbrellas sprouted gaudily on once deserted beaches. A horde of engrepreneurs descended on the island from the mainland and set up bars, shops and restaurants. House and land prices rose to unbelievable levels. Friends of ours estimated that the price they were being asked for a ruined stable on an acre of stony land was higher than the cost of a medium-sized chateau in France.

In Parosporos our old house, Villa Ariadne, once alone among the vines and lemon-trees, is now a suburban house with an enormous solar-heating panel on the roof, surrounded by modern apartments built by the grandchildren of Elias. "Our" private beach at Delfini has a busy restaurant and bodies lie out in bronzed rows on sun loungers. The road past the villa throbs with farting motor-bikes and speeding cars all day long and most of the night. Elias and Maria could not stand the noise and have moved into a quiet back street in Parikia.

On summer evenings when we sit, with old island friends, Greek and foreign, on our terrace overlooking the valley of Isterni the talk inevitably turns to the good old days, not so long ago, before the island changed forever. Bemoaning the losses, it is hard to think of any gains in the metamorphosis of Paros.

The road we can see below us, snaking its concrete way through the valley towards Naoussa was tarred and widened with EC money in the mid-1980s. The rutted track that Penelope and I jolted along that day to find

Petra and Isterni has become one of the main roads on the island, a Monte Carlo racing-track for dare-devil young men on their screaming, high-powered motor-bikes. Isterni, which used to be a remote place that even many Parians did not know, is now marked on the tourist maps. And hundreds of tourists, lost on hired mopeds, make the dead- end journey up here looking for a road to a beach.

The local council has scarred the hillside above our house with a new road which they hope will open up the place for development. Electricity poles, transformers and telephone-lines deform the landscape, marching like invading soldiers with tall lances on the very brow of the hills. Last year the electricity company attached street lamps to the poles in Isterni so that the place now looks like a fairground and Zacharias can no longer pick out our once solitary light on the hill and reassure himself that we have arrived for another summer.

On our once-quiet terrace, where the only sound we ever heard was the occasional bleating of goats, or the clamour of cicadas on still hot days, we are now assailed from the valley far below by the noise of motor-bikes, cars and jeeps whining their way to the beaches during the day and roaring drunkenly back from the bars and discos at night. The hill behind our house acts like a sounding board, making the whole valley an amphitheatre of noise. The peace we shared with the bees in the humming thyme-bushes and with the majestically-patrolling kestrels and hawks has been fractured.

On nights when the wind is blowing towards the mountain and all the unwelcome cargo of cacophony is carried with it to our terrace and into our bamboo-ceilinged bedroom, I become upset and angry. Rory, who likes noise no more than I do, is more philosophical about it. More pragmatic too. He reminds me that this noisy invasion is really only during the month of August and he is right.

There is the consolation that the high season is getting shorter each year and is only frenetic for four or five weeks. Tourism is fickle. Turkey is cheaper now, and as picturesque in most people's eyes. The decline in numbers of tourists coming to Greece over the past three years is in the order of twenty to thirty percent. This is, of course, a problem for the Parians have come to depend on tourism as their sole source of income. In the heady days of the tourist boom far too many bars, restaurants and discos were opened, a great deal too many tourist rooms were built, and too many supermarkets opened. It was a unsustainable level of growth and the signs of the ebb of tourism are evident in the abandoned nightclubs, the number of rooms to let in the high season and the half-empty restaurants in high summer.

There does not seem to have been any coherent tourism development-planning for the island, and every year there are complaints that the "wrong kind" of tourists are coming to Paros: young backpackers who do not have much money to spend and what they spend is very often on beer and wine. Hopefully lessons will have been learned and some sensible planning will result.

There are very few donkeys or mules left on the island. Only a very rare farmer can be seen these days travelling to the village on his donkey, feet kicking the donkey's sides, his straw hat angled against the sun. Indeed there are not many farmers left on the island. It is easier to make money letting out rooms, renting deckchairs on a beach or running a travel agency or tourist shop. The two sons of

Stelios, from whom we bought our house and land, no longer work their father's farm. They opened a restaurant in Naoussa (with the money we paid for the house in Isterni) and make enough money in the summer months to live on for the rest of the year.

Spiros, the gnarled old father of Pandelis, who told us that everything we put up would fall down, has died and the farm has more or less died with him. Pandelis still lives on with his gentle mother, Eleni, in the farmhouse. His handsome, lugubrious face is drawn with worry and pain. He has not enough water to irrigate the crops or to feed the animals. He is distraught. For he has had to pay the price of others' progress. As more and more houses, petrol stations and builders' supply depots have been built in the Isterni valley, more and more water is used daily, with the result that the water table has fallen and now the wells on which Pandelis's farm depended are dry and do not fill up, even after torrents of winter rain. He cannot afford the cost of drilling down hundreds of metres to reach water and so his tomatoes shrivel on the stalks, the grapes wither along the vine and Pandelis is forced to buy bottled water to drink. He rarely comes up to our house now. He has no goats to herd and perhaps he is ashamed because he has no fruit or vegetables to give us.

We used to buy all our fruit and vegetables from our neighbours, only going to Naoussa to buy groceries, to collect our post or to drink a few glasses of wine in a kafeneion with friends. Little Costas, who used to come from Naoussa on his donkey every day to cultivate the fields below our house, is too old to work now. Even that powerhouse of industry, Zacharias, has done very little farming in latter years. Not enough water, not enough energy at nearly eighty and nobody to help him to

214

plough and harvest. He still makes his delicious red wine and gives us bottles of his cold-pressed virgin olive-oil every year, but no sacks of delicious potatoes as before, no big yellow melons, nor strings of garlic or sacks of onions.

Zacharias rarely goes to Naoussa now. His donkey is dead. He does not like all the dangerous traffic and he feels sick travelling in his daughter's car. His brother, Nikolas, has left his mountain farm in Isterni and moved with the still bewildered Foto, to a new villa in Ambelas, a fishing-port near Naoussa, that mushroomed in the past decade with hotels and restaurants. The two old brothers rarely meet these days. "Ach, how would I see Nikolas? My leg is stiff and I don't go anywhere much except the church on special feast-days," Zacharias says, ruefully. "Nikolas never comes here, so I don't see him more than once or twice a year. Maybe at weddings or funerals."

Where would Zacharias go in Naoussa anyway? In the tourist season there is not much room in the village for old farmers like him. The kafeneion in the harbour where they used to have a drink, a smoke, a chat with the fishermen or a game of backgammon, punctuated with the flicking of worry-beads, is now a tourist restaurant. The old residents of the village have an air of being left behind by the magic piper. They wander about looking faintly lost among the throngs of often scantily-clad tourists who cannot speak their language. I still remember the horror and disgust I saw on the faces of some old men and women during the festival of the Virgin in August about ten years ago. The chanting priests, bearing the sacred icon of the Virgin, had set off at the head of a procession through the streets of Naoussa. As the procession moved through the *plateia*, a pair of young,

215

blonde, tourist girls, wearing bikini tops and G strings walked straight through the singing congregation on their way to sit at a cafe table, seemingly oblivious of where they were or what was going on.

I wondered then if the old people regretted all the changes tourism had brought to their village; if they measured up the wealth it had brought to their children and grandchildren against the profanity of near nudity at a midday procession of the icon of the Virgin?

Back in the late 1970s when we first saw Naoussa, there were no discos, fancy restaurants or cocktail bars. The village was falling down, its backstreets desolate and unkempt, many of the houses and churches locked up or just abandoned, their owners gone to open up Greek tavernas in Melbourne or Chicago or to build more and more suburbs in Athens. It was almost impossible to phone anyone outside the island and letters took up to three weeks to arrive, even from Athens.

Now Naoussa has quadrupled in size. Many ugly, modern, cement houses and hotels are spreading out along the bay, there seem to be fancy bakeries and discos on every corner, the old men have nowhere to play backgammon and the noise from nightclubs and restaurants keeps the villagers angrily awake until dawn.

"What am I to do?" Zacharias's daughter, Arsenias, asks us plaintively. "We get no sleep at all for the whole month of August, and not too much in June or July, either. The discos don't stop till dawn and then there's all the noise of the drunks going back to their rooms and hotels. Not all foreigners, either, a lot of wild young Athenians, too. I try to keep young Paniotis away from them, but it isn't easy. Young people are so easily influenced." And then, resignedly, she shrugs a classic Greek shrug, throws up her hands and says, *"Ti na kanome?"* This translates rhetorically as, "What can one do?" with the implied answer of, "Nothing. That's life."

Arsenias benefits from the competition among the supermarkets. She can buy produce from all over the world. Her husband, Giorgos, a builder, has built a noisy cement works on Zacharias's farm. Their family has grown quite wealthy on tourism. Arsenias has a washing-machine, she has an enormous fridge-freezer, a television and a video. Her mother, Maria, washed clothes by hand at the well and kept food cool in bags lowered into the well. Zacharias and Maria got electricity just a few years ago and now they too have a large fridge-freezer and a television. They are well-informed about world disasters and commiserated with us for years about the "bombs, boom-boom, in Belfast."

Most of the native islanders have profited in some way from tourism. They are much richer in material goods. Life is certainly more comfortable, but many, like Arsenias, complain to us about the changes; they say they are not content, that their children are spoiled with too much money and contact with the "loose morals of the foreign tourists", that the young people are only interested in money, pop music, fashion and making *kamaki*.

For us foreign residents the winds of change have brought dubious blessings, too. There are at least half a dozen supermarkets in Naoussa where you can buy once unavailable and therefore luxury goods, such as tea and butter. And you can buy newspapers from most countries in Europe the day after they are published. So now you can spend more money on what used to be luxury goods and you can read all about the doom and gloom of the world almost as soon as your friends in Dublin or Frankfurt.

In 1996 there was a sudden proliferation of phone booths all over the island, on street corners, on beaches, beside remote country schoolhouses. From these hi-tech alfresco communication boxes, you can use a callcard to phone anywhere in the world. You do not have to bother going every day to look for letters in the post office. Another pleasure and meeting-place done away with.

Every seaside village on the island has suffered a similar fate to that of Naoussa. Once empty beaches are now festooned with gaudy sun-umbrellas, pedal boats, and loungers. Paros has become a major surfing centre and attracts thousands of lithe young Germans and other northern Europeans with their camper vans and brilliantly coloured sailboards which look spectacular skimming the waves like darting butterflies. Fast food outlets provide a steady odour of burgers and fries and the thump of pop music. The main town of Parikia has tripled its permanent population and there are over a hundred thousand tourists on the island in summer.

Dozens of big ferries dock in the enlarged port every day, sometimes three at the same time. Everyone speaks some English now; there are slickly-promoted private language schools everywhere. My faithful student, Damocles, has long been out of a job. There are traffic jams and parking restrictions along the main roads. In full summer Parikia is a place to be avoided by anyone not wanting to give themselves a stress headache.

In a strange kind of way, the influx of foreign money and values and the Greek unease with this has made us, our family, more accepted, even more welcome by our old Greek neighbours and friends, especially Zacharias and

Maria. It is as if they associate us with the good old days, before the plague of materialism and consumerism. We live in more or less the same style as we used to, our house is still an old farmhouse with simple furniture we made from salvage fish-boxes and sea-delivered planks of wood. We have no TV, no swimming-pool, no car, no telephone. It is as if, in turn, we have become for them a symbol of a reassuring changelessness.

"You are old Parianos, like us," Zacharias tells us. "Twenty years you have been among us and every year you come back from so far away as Ireland. You must really love Isterni to come all that way. So long a journey! So expensive! Twenty-four hours from your house in Dublin to Isterni! And the girls, so big now, so beautiful, and still they don't forget Paros, still they want to come to Isterni. Thanks be to God."

Paros is no longer a place for Lotus-eaters, it has become a place for making money as fast as possible, for interminable building, for opening more and more bars and shops, for developing a love-hate relationship with the hundreds and thousands of tourists who flood onto the island, for cursing the heedless young people who carouse through the streets all night.

Most of our friends do not come into Parikia or Naoussa at night in the summertime. We meet for dinner or parties in each other's houses in the countryside. We swim early in the morning before the hung-over tourists are awake and the beaches are littered with umbrellas. We shop early, too, to avoid the rush. We take our motor-bikes and cars off the main roads to picnic and walk in the mountain valleys which hold no attractions for the majority of the young, wind-surfing or disco-crazy tourists.

I do not want to sound too nostalgic for the "old days",

nor too selfishly glad that the tide of tourism seems to be turning. There have been many changes for the better in the lives of the people and perhaps the lessening in the torrent of tourists will result in a more holistic and considered development-plan for the island. I am happy that many people have become better-off financially, that there is now a modern hospital in Parikia, that telecommunications have greatly improved, that there are jobs for young Parianos who do not now have to emigrate to Athens or elsewhere, that rural electrification has brought fridges and the potentially broadening and educational benefits of television into many homes, that many more families can afford better education and medical care for their children.

Why do we continue to live on this particular Greek island? Why do we not go off and find a more remote place, like Paros used to be when we first came here? Why do we return like swallows each summer? Because, fortunately, the island is more than the sum of its main towns and villages and it exists outside the mad tourist peak season. Paros still enthralls us with her thyme-scented air, her gentle female curves of hills, her clear seas, her sudden breathtaking views, her remote monasteries, her courteous old people in villages like Lefkes and Prodhromos. The sharp, white light, the quintessential Greek *phos*, has not dimmed and the sea still swells, blue and refreshing. And our dear old neighbours' annual welcome is as warm as ever. All this keeps us coming back.

Paros is an ancient island, she has lived through many invasions in the past and she will survive this late twentieth-century invasion. Life on the island cannot be lived in a museum, and change, with all its challenges and losses, is as much a part of life here as elsewhere. Swallows return to their old nesting-places year after year, as long as they can fly and the places still exist. Swallows do not mind that the horses on the farm have long since been replaced by machines or that the children who welcome their return play on computers instead of with spinning tops.

The Brennan family has put down tap-roots among the dry-stone walls of our mountain home in Isterni. Such roots are notoriously hardy and impossible to tear out.

The End